Read Aloud Magic

Give Your Child the 'Gift' of Knowledge!

Accelerate your child's vocabulary, language
and literacy development using simple
and effective methods that offer a lifetime
of benefits...in only 10 minutes a day.

Second Edition

Susan Frankenberg

Read
Aloud
Magic

Read Aloud Magic

Copyright © 2009, by Susan Frankenberg.

Second Edition

Published by:

Read Aloud Magic, LLC
944 Signal Road, Signal Mountain, TN 37377, U.S.A.
info@read-aloud-magic.com
http://www.Read-Aloud-Magic.com

Printed in the United States of America.

ISBN 978-0-615-32091-5

This book is available at quantity discounts for bulk purchases.
Contact the publisher for information.

IN ORDER TO MAKE THIS BOOK EASIER TO READ

I typically refer to a child as either "he" or "she," I refer to an individual "child," and I refer to an individual "parent." However, all of the information in this book applies equally to boys and girls, and to single and multiple children. "Parent" applies to mothers, fathers, grandparents and other caregivers. And, references to "teacher" apply to any teacher, parent or others in a teaching role.

FOREWORD

"Storytelling is a very important activity between parent and child because it fires the child's imagination, it gets them thinking, and it gets the parent and child involved together."

- Dr. Richard Woolfson,
Child Psychologist

We all have convictions, and some of our convictions are so strong they actually identify who we are and help to guide us along in life. Ever since I was a young mother with three toddlers at home I've had a strong conviction about the critical need to read with our children.

For many years I read daily to my own children and I cherish those memories. I've also read daily to the hundreds of children I've had the privilege of teaching throughout my teaching career. And, I've enjoyed sharing the joy of Reading Aloud with the adults I've met along the way – many of whom have adopted Read Aloud with their own children.

Furthermore, I have observed, both as a parent and as a professional educator, a connection between parents who consistently read with their children and the academic success of those children.

Now, I'm able to share my knowledge and experience

with you. Read Aloud is one of life's treasures and my goal is to help you get started, and help you succeed, as you strive to learn more about Read Aloud and positively impact your child's future.

Hopefully, by the time you finish reading this book you will understand how Read Aloud can change your child's academic self-confidence and accelerate his scholastic achievement. And, I hope you'll see just how easy it is to get a Read Aloud program started with your child, just as I did many years ago!

Long-term Read Aloud success is largely the result of a consistent daily Read Aloud habit. Just 10-minutes of daily Read Aloud time from birth to age five totals over 300-hours of high-quality enrichment for a child. And, there's no need to stop at age five. As Read Aloud continues beyond age five the benefits also continue.

This book, *Read Aloud Magic,* is here to help you. You may decide to read the entire book in a day or a weekend. Or, you may read a page or two a day over a more extended period of time. Either reading method will work. But, whatever you do, DON'T WAIT TO GET STARTED! The great thing about Read Aloud is that you can get started immediately. There's no benefit to waiting. In fact, every day you delay is a lost learning opportunity for your child.

ABOUT THE AUTHOR

"There are many little ways to enlarge your child's world. Love of books is the best of all."

- Jacqueline Kennedy

Susan Frankenberg is a professional educator and author, a seasoned parent and grandparent, and a life-long Read Aloud advocate. She has taught and nurtured hundreds of elementary and middle school students and she has raised three children from infancy to adulthood, arguably with excellent results. Throughout all of these years Read Aloud has been an important part of her child-rearing philosophies and her ongoing day-to-day activities.

Susan received her Bachelor of Science in Elementary Education from the University of Tennessee and graduated with Academic Honors. She has been certified to teach in the states of Tennessee, Georgia and Connecticut and her 20-year teaching career has included working with a diverse cross-section of students spanning grades 3 through 8, including experience meeting the varied needs of Special Education students.

Susan received an "Outstanding New Classroom Teacher Award" from the Hamilton County Education

Association. She has also been recognized by graduating high school students as "one of the teachers who most influenced their educational experiences." She has participated in The Tennessee Governor's Academy of Teachers of Writing. And, she has developed a reading and creative writing enrichment workshop for elementary school students.

Susan's greatest joys in teaching have involved the nurturing of students to not merely understand, but to enjoy learning and growing in the areas of literature, poetry, creative writing, and her greatest passion of all, reading. Additionally, she has served as a school facilitator for Read Aloud, working with parents as well as students to promote the joys of reading.

Susan currently teaches fourth grade at Lookout Elementary School in Lookout Mountain, Tennessee. She still has a passion for reading and a genuine love of books. She's been known to spend hours in the children's section of local bookstores looking for that special book that will spark interest in one of her students. And, if you visit her classroom, you'll find a vast selection of literature that strives to relate to the interests and needs of virtually all of her students.

ACKNOWLEDGMENTS

"Children are made readers in the laps of their parents."

- Emilie Buchwald

I wish to thank my three wonderful children, Jenni, Paul and Chris, for being my Read Aloud buddies for many years. "Jenni, our many walks in *Jennifer's Walk* were truly a foundation to the incredibly caring and wise woman you have become. Paul, other people immediately feel your sincerity and genuine interest in them. I think anyone knowing *Frog and Toad* would not be surprised to know it was one of your favorites long ago. And Chris, you're all about joy. The 'joy factor' you've been to our family reminds me of the one Max provides to the reader in *Where the Wild Things Are*."

Now, I have three new Read Aloud buddies, Lucy Mae, Emma Kate and Lily Claire, my precious granddaughters. I am blessed to have you anxiously climbing up onto my lap for a Read Aloud adventure. I wonder which books will imprint upon your lives? I love you all, "To the stars and back!"

Thanks also to my husband, Paul, for being so positive, and for helping me and supporting me throughout this entire project. I love you dearly.

I also want to offer many thanks to my previous students. Repeatedly, your enthusiasm and your positive comments, both then and now, support the importance of Read Aloud. I am so glad we were able to share so many adventures together. Your comments and letters over the years have proved to me how critically important Read Aloud really is.

Jim Trelease, we first met many years ago! I was among a very small group of moms who came to listen to you at the Agawam, Massachusetts Public Library as you were beginning your Read Aloud career. I went home that very night, gathered my three children from their beds and began reading to them daily. I know you made a difference in their lives, and you certainly made a difference in mine. I will be forever grateful that our paths crossed when my children were very young.

I also want to extend a heartfelt "thank you" to all of the teachers who still read to their students daily. You are making a huge difference in their lives and in their future. I urge you to continue making Read Aloud a priority within your incredibly hectic day.

And last but certainly not least, I would like to dedicate this book to parents everywhere who are committed to the long-term mental, physical and spiritual development of their children and who are using Read Aloud to support their child development goals. I honor and salute you all.

CONTENTS

"Reading is to the mind what exercise is to the body."

- Joseph Addison

FOREWORD   *i*

ABOUT THE AUTHOR   *iii*

ACKNOWLEDGMENTS   *v*

CONTENTS   *vii*

INTRODUCTION   *1*

WHY READ ALOUD?   *5*

READ ALOUD BASICS   *19*

GET STARTED TODAY!   *37*

THE TV CHALLENGE   *43*

CREATING A BOOK-FRIENDLY HOME   *55*

READING TIPS FOR PARENTS   *61*

     The Five Essential Components of Reading   *61*

     How Can I Help My Child Be Ready to Read and Ready to Learn?   *63*

     Simple Strategies for Creating Strong Readers   *65*

How Do I Know a Good Early Reading
Program When I See One?   *66*

A CHILD BECOMES A READER: Birth to Preschool   *69*

   The Building Blocks of Reading and Writing   *71*

   Infants and Toddlers: Birth through Age 2   *74*

   Preschoolers: Ages 3 and 4   *80*

   Some Helpful Terms to Know (Basic)   *87*

A CHILD BECOMES A READER: Kindergarten to Grade 3   *91*

   The Building Blocks of Reading and Writing   *93*

   Kindergarten   *100*

   First Grade   *112*

   Second and Third Grades   *124*

   Some Helpful Terms to Know (Advanced)   *138*

READ ALOUD BOOK RECOMMENDATIONS   *143*

RESOURCES AND BIBLIOGRAPHY   *169*

A SIMPLE TRUTH

The more you read,

the more you know.

The more you know,

the smarter you grow.

The smarter you grow,

the stronger your voice,

When speaking your mind

or making your choice.

- Author Unknown

INTRODUCTION

"The things I want to know are in books. My best friend is the man who'll get me a book I haven't read."

- Abraham Lincoln

Let's talk about your child.

Let's talk about your child's vocabulary development. Let's talk about your child's literacy development. Let's talk about your child's academic potential. And, let's talk about the overall level of success you'd like your child to achieve in school and in life.

In addition, let's talk about you and your ability to shape your child's mind and contribute to his or her academic success. And last but not least, let's talk about the powerful tool that you're currently holding in your hands offering you the potential to positively impact your child's future.

I've written this book, *Read Aloud Magic*, as a way to come into your home and talk with you about all of these things. I want to talk with you about Read Aloud and I want to do it in a simple, conversational manner. I want to share the knowledge and the insight that I've obtained throughout my personal life and my professional career. And, I don't want to complicate matters by giving you a lot of unnecessary details.

Read Aloud Magic has been written to reflect my deep-seated passion for Read Aloud. It is filled with information that you can immediately put to use. It contains valuable insight and practical tips. It is written in a simple and easy-to-understand format. And, it's been written specifically for parents like you who want to better understand the Read Aloud opportunity and how to effectively introduce it into their child's life.

I urge you to read this book and use it as your Read Aloud primer. Use it as you begin your Read Aloud journey. And, keep it as a long-term Read Aloud resource.

With these thoughts in mind, let's strive to keep our conversation clear and simple. Let's define the full scope of Read Aloud and discuss why it's such a powerful tool. Let's talk about how you can get Read Aloud started in your home. Let's address some of the challenges you may face. And last but not least, let's provide you with some of the important information that you'll need as you and your child continue down the road to long-term Read Aloud success.

One last point. Many parents ask me if their child must be a bookworm, or become a bookworm, for Read Aloud to succeed. The answer is, "No, bookworms are not expected nor required!" Read Aloud will simply be one of many focal points within your child's formative years. However, I do believe that developing an enjoyable reading habit during these formative years will enhance your child's development on many fronts. And, enhanced reading skills and heightened reading enjoyment are among the many benefits that will last for a lifetime.

My goal is to help an ever growing number of parents get started with Read Aloud – and succeed with Read Aloud. And, by doing this, we'll collectively impact an ever increasing number of children with potentially life-changing benefits.

It is my most sincere hope that today will be the day that <u>you</u> begin a Read Aloud program with your child. Don't worry about yesterday. Get started today. I can assure you, both you and your child will benefit immensely from the experience.

Read Aloud is one of the greatest gifts you can give to your child. In addition, Read Aloud will allow you to spend ongoing, quality time with your child – time that I assure you will provide a lifetime of memories. You may not see it yet. But, please trust me when I tell you, "The time you invest in Read Aloud with your child will ultimately prove to be a wonderful gift that you also give to yourself."

Now, let's get started!

WHY READ ALOUD?

"Reading to children not only builds stronger relationships, but is also considered to be the most important thing you can do to help your child succeed."

- National Literacy Trust

Children may arrive for their first day of school with their backpacks filled with pencils and other supplies. However, much of what each child really brings into the classroom that day has little to do with the items tucked inside their backpack.

As each child walks through the door and into their classroom they bring with them the collective total of all the "educational moments" that have occurred throughout their life. For many children, the collective total of these educational moments provides them with a significant academic advantage. Unfortunately, too many other children have had too few educational moments in their life and they start school at a definite disadvantage. Missing pencils can be remedied in an instant, but the educational moments missing in a child's life are not so easily replaced.

There are many reasons for inconsistencies in each child's background and educational moments. But, regardless of the reasons, they do exist. And, if you're a parent looking for a way to provide a substantially greater number of educational moments for your child, if you want to give your child a meaningful head start in school and in life, then you need to take action. The clock is ticking. But, you have many questions. What are the options? What works and why does it work? What is the short-term and long-term cost? Where do I get information that I can trust? How do I get started? And, more.

It may come as a surprise to you, but Read Aloud provides the perfect solution to this parenting challenge. It's universal. It's effective at any child's age. It doesn't matter who you are or where you live. You can get started at any time. The timing is extremely flexible and will adapt to the needs of your family. It's a low cost activity that will accommodate any budget. You set the pace and you customize your activities to fit the needs and the interests of your child. And most important of all, Read Aloud works! The life-long vocabulary, literacy and enrichment benefits of Read Aloud are very real. And, there are other benefits as well.

Read Aloud is one of the most effective tools available to help your child build a sturdy foundation in language and literacy. Understanding that letters make words, words create stories, and how to use vocabulary are essential skills that Read Aloud provides. Each time you read a book to your child he is introduced to new places, situations, people and ideas. He sees pictures of objects that are new to him. These pictures and words are logged into the child's memory. The simple act of reading a book to a child is like a mini-lesson in Language Arts.

Read Aloud can provide many benefits for a child, from the beginning of life, and help you accomplish the following with your child:

- Increase school success.

- Provide background knowledge.

- Improve listening skills.

- Promote a love of reading.

- Boost self-confidence.

- Enrich family life.

- Stimulate your child's brain.

- Strengthen family values.

- Enhance the bond between parent and child.

- Influence generations to come.

All of these opportunities can be realized with just ten minutes of daily Read Aloud time.

Read Aloud Increases School Success

If a child learns how to speak, knows his alphabet and can write his name, parents often think their job is done. Off to kindergarten the child goes. This is not so. Parents are a child's first teacher, and the most important teacher of all.

A child who has been read to has a history with books,

so he is equipped to easily plug into reading and learning. Listening has already been mastered and is easy for him. Previous books and stories will aid him in the comprehension of new ones. His brain is wired to associate reading with pleasure. Most importantly, the English language will be a comfortable tool that he can begin using like a skilled artisan.

All academic areas benefit from Read Aloud. A child who has been consistently read to throughout his early years has many advantages in school:

- His cognitive ability has been changed forever.

- His mental condition has been permanently stimulated.

- He has been intellectually fed.

- His subconscious holds messages from wise, truthful and valuable books.

Read Aloud Provides Background Knowledge

The foundation for an entire learning career is formed long before a child even enters kindergarten. Most teachers can recognize the degree of a student's "background knowledge" during the first week of school, if not the first day.

Every time you read a book to your child, his mind is filled with background knowledge and his language development is reinforced. These 10-minute segments of Read Aloud time are vital to his language development.

Read Aloud Improves Listening Skills

Reading to your child for just 10-minutes a day

translates to approximately 180 hours of reading by age three. By age five, it accumulates to approximately 300 hours of language and listening. That is 300 hours spent nourishing your child's brain! The child is a developed listener before entering school because listening skills have been built.

Many children today struggle with their attention skills. Teachers cannot solve this problem alone – parents are a child's primary teacher and role model. Reading to your child at home teaches your child how to listen. This "listening practice" will give your child a better chance of becoming an enthusiastic and successful listener.

As a teacher, I find it impossible not to notice the correlation between students whose parents practice Read Aloud and those who do not. Children who are read to at home love Read Aloud time at school – they get excited about it. They want to know what book we will read next in class. They enthusiastically summarize their reading. They enjoy Read Aloud with "involved" brains that have learned how to listen. On the other hand, children who have not had the advantage of Read Aloud also stand out. They squirm, fidget and play. They watch the clock because their ears are essentially "turned off." They have not been trained to listen and it is so very apparent.

Read Aloud Promotes a Love of Reading

Self-confidence leads to a healthy and happy mind and is reinforced whenever a children feels capable of achieving. When a child enjoys doing something she will be more likely to succeed at it. And, as a general rule, children who read well likewise enjoy reading. Therefore, if you want your child to learn to read well, give her a boost. Help her learn letters, sounds and words. Help her expand her vocabulary. Help her learn to read and then help her grow in terms of her overall reading skills. Engage her mind and imagination through stories, poetry and books. It just makes good, common sense to utilize daily Read Aloud as a key teaching and learning tool.

I am not suggesting that every child must be a bookworm. However, I encourage you to create a "book friendly" home environment that views books positively. Children who have been surrounded by books at home do not feel threatened by reading in school. Ideally, a child will enter school having spent many hours listening to stories in a warm, nurturing and "cuddled up" environment.

Consider the child who is not so comfortable around books. He enters the school library and feels overwhelmed instead of excited. He is given a science textbook and feels unprepared to tackle it instead of excited about looking through it. He has missed the crucial step to successful reading – the influence Read Aloud provides.

Children from active Read Aloud homes have seen, heard, felt and touched books all their lives. Most likely, they associate reading with a warm couch and a loved one next to them. A child who is consistently read to will never forget that loving and caring Read Aloud environment. Reading together can create a lifetime of memories between loved ones. It is like a secret place you have visited together. All this becomes associated with books in just 10-minutes a day. It is truly magic!

Read Aloud Boosts Self-Confidence

I have seen it year after year in the classroom. When a child learns to enjoy reading it follows that she will become a good reader. A self-confident reader tackles books with ease rather than fear.

Many parents encourage their children to succeed in sports. Sports can help develop healthy bodies and minds as well as boost self-confidence in children. Children learn how to be team players through sports, which is an essential part of life. If reading received the same level of attention that sports receive then parents would see amazing results!

Most parents know that you can't just put a child out onto a playing field and expect him or her to "automatically" develop superior playing skills and "automatically" have a wonderful life experience. It takes time and effort to achieve superior results. A child must prepare for success. And, this applies to his mental capabilities as well as physical capabilities.

Consider how a child typically becomes highly proficient in a sport:

- The child is introduced to the sport.

- The child is equipped for the sport.

- The child is coached in the sport.

- The child must practice the sport – including all required skills.

- The child is encouraged to overcome obstacles as he

works to develop the skills necessary for success.

- The child receives positive reinforcement whenever he plays the sport and performs well.

- The child watches more experienced players.

- Ongoing repetition is a key requirement for an ever-increasing skill level.

I think most parents would also agree that the following behaviors would frustrate a child learning a new sport or skill:

- Criticism of his capabilities or performance.

- Lack of proper preparation.

- Unjustified demands to perform beyond his skill level.

- Lacking the necessary equipment.

- Inadequate preparation.

- Frequently cancelled training sessions and practice games.

- Limited opportunities to watch accomplished players perform.

All of these issues, positive and negative, will contribute to the success or failure of a child in a chosen sport. And, you can easily apply these very same issues, both positive and negative, to your child's vocabulary development, literacy development, and other aspects of his or her physical and mental growth.

Here's the point. A child who continuously experiences

Read Aloud is being supplied with many of the tools necessary to succeed in school and in life:

- Read Aloud accelerates a child's literacy development and overall intellectual growth.

- Read Aloud contributes to a child's long-term academic success.

- Aloud stretches a child's mind and imagination.

- Read Aloud introduces a child to the many wonders of the world far beyond his or her normal day-to-day boundaries.

- Read Aloud fosters a love of books and a love of reading within a child.

- Read Aloud contributes to increased self-confidence.

- Read Aloud encourages positive growth in a parent-child relationship, creating memories that last forever.

- Read Aloud has the potential to deliver an entire lifetime of benefits.

Of course, you have the ability to withhold Read Aloud from your child. However, if you do that you are closing the door to greater success and greater opportunities for your child. The same principles that apply to sports, as we previously discussed, also apply to preparation for academic success. A child who has not had the benefits of Read Aloud may experience a variety of challenges resulting in frustration and disappointment:

- If his skills are lower than other students' skills in the classroom.

- If he is forced to read and is not comfortable with it.

- If he is expected to perform as well as the other students with higher skill levels.

- If he has little or no background knowledge of books.

- If he feels reading is a chore.

- If he must turn to television as a primary entertainer or pacifier.

Read Aloud Enriches Family Life

Read Aloud with your child can, and will, turn into one of those "I'm so glad I did that" series of events in your life.

I believe reading to my own children made a huge difference in their lives and abilities. It also made a huge difference in my life because I will forever hold dear the memories of reading to them – snapshots of time I would not trade for anything. Even as adults, they still reference stories and books they remember and that have influenced them.

Now my husband and I spend time reading to our three granddaughters. In fact, one night when we were babysitting our two older granddaughters, my husband asked them if they wanted to read. I watched as they squealed and ran to gather books in their arms. They climbed into his lap with handfuls of books. I do not know who was happier, Grandpa, the girls or me watching. I am so thankful that reading means fun to them.

In addition, our newest granddaughter, Lily, was read to on the day she came home from the hospital, and nearly every day since. She has already begun her Read Aloud journey.

Read Aloud Stimulates a Child's Brain

When a child watches television images are created for him. This is called "imposed imagery." It involves very little thinking. For the most part, the brain takes a nap while the television is on. Most of us have heard, or said, that we watch television when we feel "brain dead" or do not want to have to think. What a dramatic, adverse impact too much of this "brain dead" activity can have on a child's developing mind.

On the other hand, when a child is listening to a story she creates a movie set in her mind. This is called "induced images," which means capturing the words, interpreting them, and then producing an ongoing image. In her mind, the characters, scenery and actions are all her own. This involves work, which is good for young minds. This is why seeing a movie based on a book is not the same as actually reading the book. In a movie someone else has done the work for you. The images conjured up in your own mind through reading are typically far more detailed and personal to you than could ever be portrayed on the screen.

Read Aloud Strengthens Values

Research today tells us that children with poor values cannot learn as well as their peers who have healthy values presented daily in their homes. Public schools are now teaching character education along with reading, math and writing.

It is apparent that traditional values in American society have dramatically declined over the last ten or so years. Today's parents are required to control so many more aspects of their children's lives in order to protect them from declining moral standards and values. This is particularly apparent on television. Parents can no longer allow children to watch television unsupervised because of the questionable values that are presented. It is becoming more difficult to find quality children's programs even though the number of television channels we have access to have skyrocketed.

Read Aloud Creates a Bond between a Parent and Child

When you take time to sit and read to your child you are giving her a clear message of "you matter to me." Even the reluctant reader may resist Read Aloud at first, but never assume that she does not want or need the attention.

While reading to your child you are putting the world in second place and your child in first place. That is great insurance for a parent-child bond that lasts. If your child is used to listening to you read and share stories, and used to that feeling of comfort of just being with you, just think what an advantage you will have when they are teenagers.

Read Aloud Influences Generations to Come

My grandmother, Ruth, read to her children a lot. My dad, who is now in his eighties, still talks about those many special moments with his mother. I'd bet that Ruth was read to as a child. And, I'm certain that I was read to as a child because of Ruth. Now, I've become a strong Read Aloud advocate, too.

Isn't it amazing how such things can pass through generations? Whenever and wherever it starts, Read Aloud can begin an extremely beneficial and potentially lasting family tradition.

A Special Read Aloud Memory

I will never forget reading *Where the Red Fern Grows* to a class of middle school students.

I knew I was going to have a tough time getting through a particularly emotional chapter. Those of you who have read this book know exactly what I mean. There I was, up in front of a bunch of teenagers, hoping I would be able to hold back my tears.

As I was reading I started to choke up, so I paused for a moment to gain my composure. I will never forget what happened next. One of the eighth-grade football players, a tough young man, walked up to the front of the class, gently took the book out of my hands and read the remaining pages to the class. There were sniffles and tears throughout the class, including my own, as he read.

I was so moved by this young man's actions. It was what I call a "sacred moment" in teaching. I am certain that many of the students from that class will remember that moment for the rest of their lives.

I am grateful to have so many of these sacred moments from teaching tucked away in my memory. Read Aloud provides so many special moments of expression and thought, at home and in the classroom.

READ ALOUD BASICS

"Reading aloud with children is known to be the single most important activity for building the knowledge and skills they will eventually require for learning to read."

- Marilyn Jager Adams

We listen all day long to other people's voices but do we really pay attention to how they sound? Take a day and really listen. Listen for voices that get your attention in a positive way. What is it about someone's voice you like? Pay attention to your own voice as you speak during the day – how and why do you use expression? Of course, you take it for granted at this point in your life. It's second nature. You seldom think about it. However, to a young child you are a vocal expert, and he or she is trying very hard to learn to mimic you.

When we read to children we are playing a role. Most of us are not used to dramatizing when we read. Add a little drama to your voice next time you read out loud and notice your audience's reaction. No one would enjoy a play in which the roles were spoken with normal inflection.

Consider the voice intonations that a coach uses in sports. His tone and inflection mean so much. It can make a child like or dislike a sport. Think of yourself as your child's reading coach. Your voice, your tone and your inflections are key, and your level of enthusiasm communicates a strong message about language and about reading.

Successful Techniques for Reading to Children

- Have books available for little hands to reach.

- Display books in various places and rooms.

- Make Read Aloud time a nestled up, warm and cozy time.

- Get rid of all distractions during reading (especially the TV and cell phones).

- Let your child discuss the book while you are reading. Little ones want to point and talk about what they see.

- Incorporate any art projects or other activities you are doing at home with the books you are reading.

- Find a time that Read Aloud works and make it a habit.

- Become a storyteller rather than a word reader. You will improve with practice just as your child is learning and growing each and every time you read together.

TRY THIS . . .

Read to your child for 10-minutes a day. Read Aloud will dramatically improve his listening skills and ignite his brain. One-on-one reading is the ultimate tool to develop listening skills. It's like providing your child with a personal trainer in listening. Just by listening, your child hears words and their meaning, sentence structure, and the many tones and inflections of your voice.

Read Aloud with Babies

Some parents actually begin Read Aloud with their babies before they are born. These parents are already sold on Reading Aloud and its benefits. Babies certainly can hear before birth, so these parents take advantage of this. No doubt, these babies will be language enriched by the time they go to school.

Babies get so excited about books! Their minds are soaking in so much. First books with infants should be simple, colorful and short. They should be little, so small hands can hold them. Board books are wonderful as they don't bend or rip easily. Find some books that can even be used in the bathtub.

Babies need short books and they enjoy an exciting and stimulating narrative. They also need time to simply hold books, to discover them in their own quiet time.

Provide some board books in their "quiet time space," whether it is their crib or play area. They need to be able to touch books and begin to understand how they work. Many baby books have "touchy feely" things to stimulate tactile learning. *Pat the Bunny* is an excellent "touch" book. Babies get to feel the soft bunny fur, try on Mommy's ring and look in a mirror. In my opinion *Pat the Bunny* is an ideal book for a baby.

Talk to babies about the books you are reading. Turn

the pages with great excitement. Have you ever noticed as you're sitting in a waiting room the many different ways adults read to babies? Some just hold the book and turn the pages while others make it an adventure with a voice to match. Who would you rather have read to you?

Read Aloud with Toddlers

If you have been reading to your toddler on a regular basis you will know when she is ready for a "story" versus simply looking at pictures. When she can sit for a longer period of time and follow the pictures while you read indicates she is ready for a story.

Toddlers love to point and identify pictures they like from the books they read repeatedly. And, as in most areas of toddler life, patience is required once they latch onto a book and want to read it over and over again, even in a single sitting. The repetition is teaching your child how to predict and his sense of self-achievement is expanding. At this age a child will know if you leave out a page. He will feel proud knowing what will happen next. After all, who doesn't enjoy knowing the right answer?

With many toddlers you have to be careful of their tolerance for "scary." There are many books for toddlers that involve someone getting lost or funny monsters. Many toddlers are just fine with those while others get upset. Always read the books before you begin Read Aloud because you know what your child can handle. Be particular!

TRY THIS . . .

You may not have had a special someone who read to you. However, you can become the trigger in your family history. Create an environment in your home that makes books a priority. Then, as your children grow and mature Read Aloud will hopefully become a part of their homes and families and continue for multiple generations to come.

Read Aloud with Readers

If you are beginning Read Aloud with a school age child the first book sets the stage. Be wise in your decision. Think about a book you loved as a child. However, some great books make poor Read Aloud choices. Your first choice needs to be "the hook." Read the first page. Does it capture your attention? If not, don't use it.

Once a child begins reading on her own do not stop your Read Aloud times together. Unfortunately, too many parents make this mistake. They somehow have gotten the mistaken impression that Read Aloud is only for non-readers. However, Read Aloud is definitely for readers, too. In fact, characters and plots are more developed at this stage so you have just begun the fun!

Where do you begin picking out Read Aloud books for children who can read? Choose books above your child's reading level. For example, if your child is reading at 1st grade level, then pick out books that are at perhaps at 3rd grade level. When I read to my 4th grade students I usually pick books at least at a 5th or 6th grade reading level.

Why do we do this? We want to stretch their brains as they listen. Their brains are capable of understanding so much more than what they can actually read. We want to stretch their vocabulary. We do not talk to children in their "reading ability" language so why would we read to them at that lower level? The same goes for the little ones. Read books to them that are above their reading ability level.

Beginning Reader books are great for learning to read. Let your child read these out loud to you. However, many kindergarteners and beginning readers are capable of listening to books such as *Charlotte's Web*, which is a third or fourth-grade reading level book.

"Selling" Read Aloud to Your Child

A parent's job is often one of "sales associate." In the case of Read Aloud your job is to sell the idea that "books are valuable." You want your child to want you to read the book you are holding. You want them to look forward to the opening of the book. The child who catches this anticipation has a huge advantage in school. He has caught the idea that books are special, thus school and books are viewed positively rather than neutral or negatively.

Here is a short analogy to clarify the role that a parent can play in helping their child achieve more through Read Aloud. The analogy is based on football, but the principles are much the same.

First, imagine a boy showing up for football try-outs after being told by his parents to get out there and play. He's never played organized football before. He's watched some football on television but no one has ever taken the time to teach him the game. He's not in shape, he doesn't understand the team positions and he doesn't understand the rules of the game. Obviously, he has never had a reason to develop a real sense of excitement about football.

Now, imagine another football newcomer showing up for these same try-outs. His parents have been talking about football with him from as far back as he can remember. They have played it with him and taken him to games. He has pictures in his room about football. They discuss it in a positive manner at meals. Together they went to pick out his uniform, letting him wear it before his first practice. They took his picture in it. They have sold him on the idea of football. He's excited about football.

Other things being reasonably equal, which of these two boys do you think stands the best chance of winning a position on the team? The answer is obvious. And, the same rules apply to the approach we take with our children regarding reading and school.

When we entice children to participate in reading at a very young age they quickly pick up our attitude. If you approach reading with a "you have to do this" stance, you are doing more harm than good. You have to sell it in a positive framework.

Next, let's go to the first day of school and in walks Jane, a product of Read Aloud parents. She has heard thousands upon thousands of words read to her in her young life. The comfort and pleasure of reading have been deeply imprinted. Reading is something she wants to do because she is comfortable with it. Animals, colors, characters, places and literally thousands of other ideas are stored in her brain. Jane feels confident in school due to her background knowledge. School becomes fun and comfortable because she is familiar with what is found there.

In contrast, let's take a look at Ann, another young girl on here first day at the same school. However, Ann does NOT have a Read Aloud background. She has NOT spent hours upon hours of reading or listening. She does NOT have a connection with books or with reading

Unfortunately, the contrasts between Jane and Ann are also quite obvious. Ann finds it more difficult than Jane to follow along in class. Ann gets easily distracted during reading times, fidgeting and squirming whenever she becomes lost with whatever is going on. When books are read Ann has a difficult time grasping the thoughts expressed by the words. Comprehension is low. And as a result, Ann begins to feel less and less confident in the classroom.

Clearly, there is a significant difference in Jane's and Ann's background due to Jane's Read Aloud experiences. And, that difference shows up right away in the classroom. Jane's parents have positioned her for academic success while Ann has considerable catching up to do. Of course, this example may be an over simplification. But, it does illustrate one of the key benefits of Read Aloud – increased academic success.

TRY THIS . . .

Your home can help to ensure your success. Stack it full of books and use them as an insurance policy for success. Make your home book friendly, and therefore school friendly, right from the start. Talk positively about school and learning before your child starts school. Most importantly, try to spend 10-minutes of Read Aloud time with your child each and every day.

Approaching a Reluctant Reader

Perhaps you have a child who dislikes reading. If so, he is probably not among the top arena of readers at school. Don't worry. You can still create a reader. I've seen it happen many times.

Reluctant readers CAN get hooked on books. There are reasons he might be a reluctant reader, and the reasons include:

- Reading has been a struggle for him in school.

- He has never experienced great books.

- No one has ever offered Read Aloud.

- Books are not part of his life.

- He has developed poor reading habits and has had poor success with reading in school.

Deal with a reluctant reader carefully. The first approach you take will set the climate for Read Aloud, so think it through. How would you want someone to approach you with the intent to "sell" an idea to you?

Here are some tips that you can use when you are approaching a reluctant reader:

- Have a positive attitude, thus setting the atmosphere.

- Ask questions, because everyone likes to talk.

- Encourage opinions – and listen to them!

- Talk about how Read Aloud will benefit them.

- Be interested in your child.

- Talk about Read Aloud when you can focus on the topic and really listen and respond to your child's thoughts.

Also, be creative in the methods you use as you reach out to your potential reader:

- Set books around the house and pick one up when your non-reader seems available. Pick a time when both of you have a moment alone, "Hey, listen to this!"

- Find a short age-appropriate editorial that you know he will find interesting and hopefully have an opinion about.

- Find a magazine that will get his attention and leave it out on the kitchen table.

- Bathrooms work well – put a basket in there and fill it.

- Keep a basket of books in the car for trips around town.

- Talk about articles, books or magazines to others while the "reluctant one" is around. If you know one of his friends likes to read you have a marketing gold mine. We know how influential friends can be – use it as a benefit.

- Many picture books are actually at 4th and 5th grade reading levels. Some reluctant readers will begin to feel successful after finishing a very short book as long as they don't feel like they are reading below their grade level.

- I carefully choose books for reluctant readers. Find out what their interests are and go from there. Do they love animals or nature? Do they get excited by trucks, airplanes or space ships? Are they involved in sports? Are mysteries an interest for them? Do they love the beach or the mountains? Begin with a topic that interests and excites them.

- Don't forget about nonfiction. Perhaps the most reluctant reader I have known was hoping to be a pilot someday. So, when he was handed a real pilot's flight training manual he instantly went from a non-reader to avid reader. He simply needed something meaningful to him to spark his interest.

One of the first things I do each school year is to have a "book advertisement" time. My students do not know I call it this. I simply ask if anyone has read a great book. I always have some students who cannot wait to share what they have read. (This is peer pressure at its best!) Then, I "just happen" to have a pile of winners nearby that I casually ask if anyone has read. I do a short sell on each, and read a little bit from a few. I pick sections that grab their attention and then I stop just when it gets good – a tactic taken from television.

The key is to find things that will interest the reluctant reader and then make those types of things accessible and normal to have around. You can make books a natural part of your family's environment even if they haven't been in the past.

TRY THIS . . .

Create a safe and educational environment for your children through Read Aloud. Always read books before you buy them to check out the values they teach. Talk with your child about the books that you read. Be choosy about what your child reads. And, be VERY careful about what she watches on television.

Choosing a Read Aloud Time

Finding quality Read Aloud times with your infant or toddler is relatively easy. Obviously, full tummies and warm snuggly places work best. Either sit them in your lap or have them cuddled up to you with their dominant hand between you and the book. If they seem to be right handed sit on their right side. If they tend to favor their left hand sit on their left side. Try it yourself. Have someone read to you from both sides and see which side makes you feel most comfortable. Make Read Aloud times short and use your voice. Make it a fun time to look forward to.

Keep books within reach – and keep them everywhere! For instance, keep a basket of books within reach of the car seat. Your child can look at books in her car seat and you can grab one if you know you will be anywhere with a wait (such as a doctor's office or restaurant). There are so many minutes in a day that can be filled with a story if you simply make it a point to plan ahead.

Read Aloud time is quality time spent with your child. Make sure your child knows you are making this time a priority. Let her see you turn off your cell phone. Dishes can wait. When you are 80, will you regret that household chores were not done promptly or will you cherish the moments you got to spend reading with your child?

School-age children typically have a variety of time commitments. Therefore, it may work best within your family to spend Read Aloud time in the morning before school starts. After school is usually a good time for children to play and exercise. Bedtime is another good time for Read Aloud as it provides a comforting experience right before a child goes to sleep.

TRY THIS . . .

Whether it is sports or reading, positive reinforcement and continuous parental encouragement make for success. Reading to children develops their ability to work successfully within the school community and promotes a lifestyle of academic success. Spend 10-minutes a day in Read Aloud with your child.

The Read Aloud Bedtime Ritual

Reading at bedtime is a tradition you might want to begin for a number of excellent reasons:

- Bedtime is a predictable time for Read Aloud that your child can look forward to.

- Drifting off to sleep while someone reads to you is a comforting way to go to bed.

- Read Aloud at bedtime relaxes your child, providing a better night's sleep.

- Read Aloud at bedtime is a very positive way to end the day – for both the parent and the child.

Think about the many ways a deep, peaceful rest at night affects a child throughout their day. A night of sound sleep in which a child drifts off being read to has to have an impact on his learning and emotional state. The benefit seems all too obvious. Compare this to a child who has drifted off to sleep to the sound of the television, which is an all too common phenomenon. Can you imagine what images they go to sleep with? It's scary to consider.

Give Your Child a Boost in School

Read Aloud time with your child will provide him with so many advantages and benefits. Imagine if your child:

- Has heard a million extra spoken words and been exposed to an untold number of illustrations.

- Has watched his language being used with expression

while being read stories that have exposed him to myriad places, adventures and persons.

- Equates reading with pleasure, cuddling up with someone who takes the time to read.

- Understands letters and words, how they work and knows where the words are coming from.

- Memorizes a story so well that just one word cannot be missed without him knowing.

Read Aloud in the Classroom

Listening is a critical part of mastering a language and it must be learned and practiced. I have worked with teachers who allow students who do not listen well to color or engage in another activity while everyone else listens to reading. I believe that everyone needs to learn to listen and pay attention – especially the poor listeners. Allowing them to do other activities is just further enabling them to remain poor listeners.

Teachers must learn to make listening exciting. That means picking books that grab their students' attention. That means using voice and body language to interpret a story. Students deserve to have the very best of Read Aloud. Teachers need to make reading come alive for their students.

Many classrooms have reading lounges – a specific area for reading. These lounges or nooks provide students with a comfortable spot to read. Some rooms have lofts filled with pillows. Even if a classroom doesn't have this kind of space students can certainly enjoy Read Aloud from their desks. Up until recently, most classrooms had no other option. That is when the storytelling part of Read Aloud becomes important – expression and movement help capture their attention.

It's Never too Late for Read Aloud

What if your child is no longer a lap-child? What if your child is now in upper elementary school? Is it too late to help? Definitely not!

I know many parents who have started Read Aloud to their children (fourth graders) and found their kids just soaked it up. The children craved the attention, and found the time comforting and reassuring. I have seen Read Aloud improve their success in school, too. I have seen students who have responded to Read Aloud and become better listeners immediately. It can be done!

Children crave their parents' attention. Sharing a good book with them for 10-minutes a day will give you about 60-hours a year of quality one-on-one time.

Smart parents choose books carefully. They explain to their children why they want to begin Read Aloud with them. They make sure the child understands the rewards, which is an important point. Of course, a young baby or toddler doesn't need to hear why Read Aloud is going to improve his life. However, an elementary school child is going to want to know what's in it for him. Therefore, it's important that you explain your reason for wanting to spend 10-minutes a day of Read Aloud time together.

Here are some of the "reasons" to use to help you "sell"

Read Aloud to your child. I'm sure you'll find ways to personalize these points as you discuss them with your child:

- School will become easier.

- Grades will improve.

- Let's share some stories together.

- It is fun!

- You are important to me and I want time with just you.

- You are worth it!

TRY THIS . . .

Grandparents and other family members can be great Read Aloud helpers. Be sure to have books at their homes, or bring some along, when you visit.

GET STARTED TODAY!

"A journey of 1,000 miles begins with a single step."

- Ancient Chinese Proverb

You and your child can experience the many benefits of Read Aloud with only 10-minutes of daily Read Aloud time. All you need is a plan, a book and 10-minutes of your time each day. Of course, you'll want to learn more about Read Aloud as you move forward. But, you don't need to be an expert to get started.

Here's your easy-to-follow road map for long term Read Aloud success:

Plan it. Do it. Repeat it tomorrow!

Pick a Time

This may seem obvious or trivial. However, it's more important than you think. Good intentions aren't enough. Good intentions fall victim to the pressures of the day. Therefore, it's very important to commit to a specific time for Read Aloud and then make every effort to honor that commitment.

Consider your full range of potential Read Aloud times. Think creatively if necessary. Read Aloud times should fit your family's schedule. Different days may require different Read

Aloud times. Other family members should be made aware of your Read Aloud time commitments. And last but not least, whatever you commit to, write it down.

Pick a Place

This goes hand-in-hand with picking a time. Plan ahead. It's important. If possible, use the coziest spot in the house.

Identify a quiet place that is away from distractions to get the maximum benefit from your Read Aloud time. You should NOT have Read Aloud in front of the television or in any area with a high level of distraction.

You probably have many excellent places available for your Read Aloud times. Of course, some places will work better than others based on your particular situation. However, the key is to allow yourself to think creatively.

These are just a few of the places to consider for your Read Aloud times. Sit on the sofa, sit on the floor or sit on a bed. Go out onto the porch or patio. Go out into the yard or go to a nearby park. Sit on the grass or under a tree. Sit in the car. Go to the library. And the list goes on. Simply consider your options and then decide.

Pick a Book

If you already have a small collection of age-appropriate children's books you're all set. Within reasonable limits, almost any book can get you started. Then, as you move forward, you'll quickly learn what types of books and stories super-charge your child's Read Aloud interests.

If you do not yet have a starter collection of books for Read Aloud, you have many options available to you. If the cost of buying books is a challenge for you in these tough economic times, don't worry. There are many ways to get started at little or no cost.

Here's a list of various sources for books to help you get started with your Read Aloud activities:

- New and used books are available 24/7 from a variety of online retailers. I'm a fan of Amazon.com, but you have many choices.

TRY THIS . . .

- Go to the Amazon.com website at www.Amazon.com.

  Select **Books** from the search box drop-down menu.

  Enter **children's books a**s your search term and click on **GO**.

  Your search results page will list various age groups to select from: Baby-Age 3, Early Readers (Ages 4-8), Middle Readers (Ages 9-12), or Teens. **Click on the desired age group**.

  Next, as you review the listings, click on any book to get more detailed information. Confirm the book's targeted age group (usually found on the book's front or back cover). Look at the sample pages inside the book. Evaluate the book's content. Look at the customer rating (up to 5 stars), read the customer reviews, carefully identify a few possibilities and then make your selection.

- Visit the children's book department in your favorite bookstore. I recommend that you always talk to a knowledgeable sales associate for age appropriate book ideas and information.

- Check-out books from your local library. Then, whenever you find a book that your child really loves and wants to read over and over you can purchase a copy and add it to your child's library.

- Borrow books from a friend or neighbor.

- Visit a "used book" bookstore.

- Go to weekend flea markets, yard sales, garage sales or tag sales. People are selling their old household belongings at near giveaway prices. Very often, you'll find children's books in very good condition for a dollar or less.

- Call or visit your local library, town hall and elementary schools and ask about low cost and free book resources available in your area.

- Investigate the availability of "Reading is Fundamental" (RIF) in your area. RIF is supported by the U.S. Department of Education and is focused on children's literacy, with free books that you can keep.

- A variety of free books are available on the Internet. You can begin by searching on any major search engine for "free children's books" and expand your search from there. Please be aware that some websites offer books that are free to read online but downloads must be purchased. Also, some Internet download books do not include pictures or graphics. Check out the free literature available at www.ProjectGutenberg.com and www.RosettaProject.org.

- If you don not have any Read Aloud story books available you can always use The Bible or other religious text as your Read Aloud starting point.

Gradually Learn More about Read Aloud

You'll want to learn more about Read Aloud as you move forward. You can research and validate Read Aloud information on your own. Or, we'll provide you with the information you need – when you need it. The choice is yours.

Read Aloud success is based on consistent Read Aloud activities. Simply focus on spending 10-minutes a day of quality Read Aloud time with your child and on achieving your Read Aloud goal for TODAY! Then do the same thing tomorrow. If you'll just focus on TODAY, every day, then your long-term Read Aloud goals will fall into place. After all, isn't that what you want? Go ahead…

Get Started TODAY!

THE TV CHALLENGE

So please, oh PLEASE, we beg, we pray,
Go throw your TV set away,
And in its place you can install,
A lovely bookshelf on the wall.

- Roald Dahl, *Charlie and*
the Chocolate Factory

What could be better that sitting with a young child in your lap watching an age-appropriate TV show or video program? We all do it. It's fun. It's relaxing. It feels like "quality time together." It's a very natural occurrence. However, I caution you to view this only for what it is – enjoyable time together. Please don't make the mistake of assuming that joint TV time in any way replaces the need to spend quality time actively supporting your child's mental and social development.

It's no secret that as a society we'd developed a deep-seated love for television. We have flat screen displays, digital technology, hundred's of channels, twenty-four hour news, sports, reality shows, endless movies, specialty programming and so much more. TV is a significant focal point in our lives. Some call it an addiction. However, despite the fact that TV is such an integral part of our lives it is important to understand that TV has no significant value as a child development tool. In fact, too much TV for any child carries serious negative consequences.

We could write an entire book about television. We could discuss how it contributes to our lives. And, we could discuss the negative consequences of television. However, that is not my purpose. Instead, I want to help you understand how television negatively impacts your child development goals. And, if you are willing to accept that fact, I want to help you manage your way through your TV challenges.

There's a tremendous body of knowledge about children and television based on thousands of studies on the subject. Here's a brief sampling of key points that child development professionals have researched and reported about children and television. Consider this:

- Scientists who study brain development widely dismiss any notion that children can learn productively by watching television.

- Social interaction is a critical part of a baby's healthy development. However, time spent watching TV replaces time spent interacting with caregivers and other children.

- Television viewing can effect a child's social development, behavior, morals, values, sleep patterns, dietary habits, weight and more.

- Television viewing replaces other healthy activities such as social interaction, play time, physical activity, use of mind and imagination, homework, reading and more.

- Simply having a TV in a child's bedroom can be linked to reduced academic skills. This is probably due to the fact that kids with a TV in their bedroom watch an average of 1.5 hours more TV per day than kids without a TV in their bedroom.

- The French Broadcast Authority wants to protect children under 3 from the effects of television by broadcasting warning messages to parents advising, "Watching television can slow the development of children under three, even when it involves channels aimed specifically at them."

What if Your Child is a TV Junkie?

I can't tell you how many times I've heard a parent acknowledge that their child watches too much television. They tell me that their child doesn't want to play sports because they would rather watch television. I've also had parents tell me that a child will hardly answer them when the television is on. I'm always amazed at this lack of parental control. It's as if they don't want to make their child the least bit "uncomfortable." They don't want to take away something that gives their child pleasure. The child is in control of being "out of control."

Researchers at Johns Hopkins Bloomberg School of Public Health found that Northern Californian third-graders (ages about 8) with televisions in their bedrooms watched more television and performed worse on standardized tests than classmates without bedroom televisions.

In almost 20-years of teaching I have never had a high-achieving student who was addicted to watching television. Conversely, I have observed a definite correlation between high television viewing levels and reduced academic success. I don't even have to ask the students about their television habits. I hear them talking about shows they watch and I learn what they do in their spare time simply by being with them for seven hours a day, five days a week. In addition, I've observed that my lower performing readers are frequently television addicts.

Of course, on a student by student basis there are many factors that impact academic performance. However, I am merely stating that well-developed reading habits have a positive impact on academic success, and well-developed television habits have a negative impact on academic success. And, most important of all, it is the parent who decides which of these two paths their child will take.

I think that we are allowing television to steal our children's creativity. It attacks their innocence. The healthy values we want our children to obtain are devalued. Hours of worthless television replaces hours that could have been spent enriching their brains through reading and Read Aloud.

If you feel your child is watching too much television, for goodness sakes, shut it off. Unplug it. There's a reason why many experts are telling parents to move the television out of their children's bedrooms.

Who is in charge here? Why would you allow your child to make decisions that are not in his best interest? Isn't it time we stop allowing network executives and advertisers to negatively influence our children? Isn't it time we let our children know we care enough about them to not allow them to waste their childhood sitting in front of a television set?

Be proactive and set some limitations immediately. Today, leading experts strongly suggest you take over your homes and more specifically, your children's television habits. We have allowed television networks to move into our homes and literally be in charge.

The decision to Read Aloud more and spend less time watching television will change a child's life forever.

Consider allowing your child to pick 30 minutes of daily television viewing that you familiar with and that you approve of. Or better yet, watch that show with your child and then, or later, talk to them about the show. Discuss the story, the characters, the locations, the weather, the humor, the happy feelings, the sad feelings and anything else that stands out as a point of discussion.

Quality Television

Young people rely on trusted adults to guide and influence them in the correct way. Children are extremely vulnerable and it is up to us, as parents, to protect them. That is why so many parents are starting to turn off or unplug the television. We don't need those influences on a child's mind.

Yet, it is easy to spend so much time protecting our

children from the world that we forget to reach them with what is good about the world. We also need to take intentional steps to reach them with positive influences. That is where activities such as Read Aloud come in.

Take the time to find appropriate, quality material for your child to watch on television.

- Turn the "script" switch ON. Your family will quickly adjust to the text and your child will begin reading the script while watching television.

- Support and tune into PBS.

- Be completely aware of what is on the television whenever your child is watching it.

- Find some quality movies that you can watch together, and discuss the movie just as you would discuss a book.

- Allow children to choose alternatives. Teach them how to make healthy decisions on their own.

Replacing TV Time

We have to do something to entice our children away from the hours wasted in front of the television. There are simply too many studies that point to the harmful effects that can occur from mindless television watching.

If needed, make a list of other activities and post them on the refrigerator or somewhere noticeable. (If possible, have your child participate in creating this list.)

My suggestion would be to get a great novel and begin

reading it. Create enriching memories through Read Aloud instead of allowing hundreds or thousands of hours to be wasted in front of the television.

If you want a great testimonial to this concept read *Gifted Hands: The Ben Carson Story* by Ben Carson M.D. It is the story of one very remarkable woman who understood the importance of reading. Her resources were very limited but her drive and determination to help her sons succeed was unyielding. This book should be read by anyone involved with children. It demonstrates how one committed person can do so much to positively affect a child's entire life.

Here's a brief summary of Ben Carson's story:

Benjamin Carson was born in Detroit, Michigan. His mother, Sonya, had dropped out of school in the third grade and married when she was only thirteen. When Benjamin was eight his parents divorced and his mother was forced to raise Benjamin and his older brother, Curtis, on her own. She worked at two jobs, and sometimes three jobs, to make ends meet.

Benjamin and Curtis did not apply themselves in school and fell far behind in their studies and in their grades. In fact, in fifth grade Benjamin was at the very bottom of his class. His classmates called him "dummy" and he had developed a violent and uncontrollable temper.

When his mother saw her two sons' ever worsening grades and lack of ambition she became determined to turn their lives around. She sharply limited their television use and would not let them go outside to play until their homework was done. In addition, she required them to read two library books every week and write a book report for every book they read. What her sons didn't know until years later was that Ms. Carson was nearly illiterate and couldn't read any of their work. However, she knew what was needed to help her boys succeed and she didn't let her own lack of education get in her way.

Within weeks of implementing these changes Benjamin astonished his classmates by identifying rock samples his teacher had brought to class. He recognized them from one of the books he had read. "It was at that moment that I realized I wasn't stupid," he later recalled. Benjamin continued to amaze his teachers and classmates with his newly found knowledge and within a year he was performing at the top of his class.

A hunger for knowledge had taken hold of Benjamin and he began to read voraciously on all subjects. He eventually decided that he wanted to become a doctor and he learned to control the violent temper that had threatened his future. After graduating with honors from high school he attended Yale University and earned a degree in Psychology.

After Yale, Benjamin attended medical school at the University of Michigan and his interests shifted from psychiatry to neurosurgery. In addition to his outstanding academic performance, Benjamin's excellent hand-eye coordination and his three-dimensional reasoning skills helped him become a superior surgeon. Following medical school Benjamin became a neurosurgery resident at the world-famous

Johns Hopkins Hospital in Baltimore. Then, at only 32 years of age, Dr. Benjamin Carson became the Director of Pediatric Neurosurgery at Johns Hopkins. This was quite an accomplishment for someone who was once performing at the bottom of his class.

This amazing mom, Sonya Carson, took the right steps and changed her sons' lives forever. Imagine their reaction when she first put the changes into effect. Next, imagine how thankful they must feel now.

The bottom line is that television and video games are not going away. However, it is up to you to decide what is healthy for your family.

Attention Deficit Problems

The *American Academy of Pediatrics* recommends that children younger than two not watch television at all. The 2004 issue of the journal *Pediatrics* offers research that determined that some attention problems were related to the number of hours spent watching television. The research showed that as viewing time increased the probability of attention-deficit problems rose.

I have been in homes where a child is "glued" to the television. Trying to get his attention is difficult as his brain has turned off all incoming stimulation and is being occupied by a show that does not require any thinking whatsoever. I relate it to putting your computer on "sleep." It is there and alive, but not working. The child sits there with input but is void of any mental processing.

Now put that same child in a classroom and he treats the teacher and incoming lessons pretty much the way he has been trained to with the hours of television viewing. Watch it with no interaction. Don't think. Let it entertain your brain with input that requires no output at all. It just will not work, and the child becomes restless and uncomfortable. He wants something to distract his brain, not stimulate it to think. That is what he has been doing for hours upon hours.

I am not for one second suggesting that television causes ADD or ADHD. I am not a doctor. Furthermore, I realize not all studies are in agreement on this subject. However, I am suggesting that if a child is showing signs of these syndromes, perhaps one of the first areas that could be considered is the amount of television he or she is exposed to.

Read Aloud versus Television

The advantages of Read Aloud versus television are many:

- Television can be watched without any effort. Reading supports imagination and creativity.

- Television requires no interaction. Reading encourages thought and language between the reader and listener.

- You have only limited control over what television presents your child. You have total control what you read to him.

- Television does not provide memories. Read Aloud makes memories.

- Some television programs may violate your values. Great books support the values you want to instill in your child.

- Television babysits while reading requires mental involvement.

- Television slows down a child's brain activity. Reading stimulates child's brain.

- Television has been proven to be a deterrent to academic success. Reading enhances a child's academic success.

CREATING A BOOK-FRIENDLY HOME

"Books are not made for furniture, but there is nothing else that so beautifully furnishes a house."

- Henry Ward Beecher

Prepare your child to be good reader by creating a reader-friendly environment at home.

Books Everywhere

"Decorating" with books does not have to be a big expense. Big baskets next to tables and chairs work well and can be moved easily. Multi-colored plastic bins can be placed on lower shelves in bedrooms and are especially good for small board books.

Share the coffee table with your children. Put out some books that you want to read together during the week. One of my most vivid memories about a neighborhood friend of mine who had two children in gifted classes was her coffee table – it was always covered in books. I am sure this contributed to how well her children did in school. Interestingly, I cannot remember where the television was in their home.

Make your child's bedroom "reading friendly." I had a young woman tell me that her sister was a big reader and she was not. She attributed this to the fact that her sister had a light next to her bed while growing up, and she did not.

Frame illustrations from some favorite books your child has enjoyed. Go to a used bookstore for second copies if you do not want to cut up the original. Some bookstores will allow you to sign up to receive book posters they display once they are done with them.

If your child loves to draw, paint and color have her illustrate her favorite book and hang it up. What a great way to encourage artistic abilities while promoting books.

I have seen more and more greeting cards with illustrations of books on the front. Those would be easy to frame and hang.

Book Spots

The television has a prominent location in many American homes. Unfortunately, many children also have televisions in their rooms. I would encourage parents to take televisions out of all bedrooms and replace them with bookshelves and books.

Keep Baskets of Books in the Car

Put a basket next to the car seat from which babies may handle books easily to look at while riding. Change the books often. Put some in safe bags so it is fun to open. Wrap some in a cloth napkin so tiny hands can open them and feel like they are a present! (Plus, cloth napkins come in handy in the car.)

Toddlers and young children can pick out which books they want to have with them in the car. Choices become important to them so give them this opportunity to make the decision. They are more apt to look at a book they have chosen. If they are learning to count specify a number of books they may take and let them try counting that many books. A box of sight word flashcards in the car will help with those tougher words.

Buy Books as Gifts

Giving books as gifts helps demonstrate how wonderful books are. Books as gifts give children the message that books are special. Let your child help pick out books for her friends.

Books make wonderful baby gifts and are a great way to introduce new parents to the importance of books. Many parents keep books in the car, a few in the diaper bag, some in the crib, and some go to grandparents' homes. Duplicates are not a problem – there can never be too many.

Books make terrific gifts for new grandparents. They are so busy getting items to help them care for the baby when it visits that they often don't think of books. The more I get into this grand-parenting adventure the more I think grandparents need baby showers, too!

Need a gift for a teacher? Books are so appreciated by educators. Ask if there's a paperback they'd like for their room. Or, give them a gift certificate for the bookstore. Trust me, they'll love it, and your child will benefit. One year, I actually had a parent give me a subscription to a children's magazine. It was a wonderful gift!

Whenever you buy a book for someone and give it to them as a gift your child will get the message that books are special enough to gift-wrap and put a bow on. That's a valuable message that will stick with a child.

Use Books as Rewards

Whether a toddler has become potty successful or an older child proud of some other noteworthy accomplishment, a trip to the bookstore makes a very positive statement if the books are a reward for a job well done.

MAKE BOOKS A TRADITION

The following are some ideas that can help you incorporate some family traditions that encourage reading:

Valentines' Day

Start each Valentines' Day with a gift-wrapped book. Write your child a loving message in it with the date.

At Christmas

Make books a part of holiday giving. Perhaps you open one special present on Christmas Eve. Start the tradition of it being a book for everyone. It gives everyone something to snuggle up with in bed as they wait for Santa.

Have someone begin a tradition of reading something special every year at Christmas or on other special days. When I was growing up my parents would read us some of my father's amateurish and quite silly poems. These times always included a lot of laughing, sometimes even before the actual reading began! It was a tradition of listening to words being read to us by someone we loved. Now, we keep those treasured poems in a notebook.

Something as simple as reading *The Night Before Christmas* every year on Christmas Eve can become a lasting memory that will associate reading with pure happiness. That is your goal – to get your children to think of reading in a positive frame of mind. Don't let the television become the only "comfort" memory in your home.

First Day of Summer Vacation

Make the day special with a trip to get books to read all summer long.

Baby Showers (at Work)

Many offices host baby showers for pregnant employees. An easy and fun way to celebrate is for everyone to chip in for a gift certificate for books. It's an easy gift to coordinate and lots of fun for the parents to pick out special books for their little one.

Baby Showers (Family)

Host a special event and ask guests to bring their favorite childhood book as a gift, with a note about why they loved it and who read it to them. These special "reading memories" from grandparents, aunts and uncles will be treasured for years to come.

READING TIPS FOR PARENTS

"There is no substitute for books in the life of a child."

- Mary Ellen Chase

The Five Essential Components of Reading

Reading well is at the heart of all learning. After all, children who can't read well, can't learn well. However, you have the power to make a difference in your child's life!

Reading with children and helping them practice specific reading components can dramatically improve their ability to read. Scientific research shows that there are five essential components of reading that children must be taught in order to learn to read. Adults can help children learn to be good readers by systematically practicing these five components:

1. Recognizing and using individual sounds to create words, or **phonemic awareness**. Children need to be taught to hear sounds in words and understand that words are made up of the smallest parts of sound, or phonemes.

2. Understanding the relationships between written letters and spoken sounds, or **phonics**. Children need to be

taught the sounds that individual printed letters and groups of letters make. Knowing the relationships between letters and sounds helps children to recognize familiar words accurately and automatically, and "decode" new words.

3. Developing the ability to read a text accurately and quickly, or **reading fluency**. Children must learn to read words rapidly and accurately in order to understand what is read. When fluent readers read silently, they recognize words automatically. When fluent readers read aloud, they read effortlessly and with expression. Readers who are weak in fluency read slowly, word by word, focusing on decoding words instead of comprehending meaning.

4. Learning the meaning and pronunciation of words, or **vocabulary development**. Children need to actively build and expand their knowledge of written and spoken words, including what they mean and how they are used.

5. Acquiring strategies to understand, remember and communicate what is read, or **reading comprehension**. Children need to be taught comprehension strategies, or the steps good readers use to make sure they understand text. Students who are in control of their own reading comprehension become purposeful, active readers.

How Can I Help My Child Be Ready to Read and Ready to Learn?

- Talk to your infant and toddler to help him learn to speak and understand the meaning of words. Point to objects that are near and describe them as you play and do daily activities together. Having a large vocabulary gives a child a great start when he enters school.

- Read to your baby every day starting as young as possible. Reading and playing with books is a wonderful way to spend special time with her. Hearing words over and over helps her become familiar with them. Reading to your baby is one of the best ways to help her learn.

- Use sounds, songs, gestures and words that rhyme to help your baby learn about language and its many uses. Babies need to hear language from a parent or other care giver. Television is little more than "noise" to a baby.

- Point out the printed words in your home and other places you take your child such as the grocery store. Spend as much time listening to your child as you do talking to him.

- Take children's books and writing materials with you whenever you leave home. This gives your child fun activities to entertain and occupy him while traveling and going to the doctor's office or other appointments.

- Create a quiet, special place in your home for your child to read, write and draw. Keep books and other reading materials where your child can easily reach them.

- Help your child see that reading is important. Set a good example for your child by reading books, newspapers and magazines.

- Limit the amount and type of television you and your child watch. Better yet, turn off the television and spend more time cuddling and reading books with your child. The time and attention you give your child has many benefits beyond helping him be ready for success in school.

- Reach out to libraries and community and faith-based organizations. These organizations can:

- Help you find age-appropriate books to use at home with your child.

- Show you creative ways to use books with your child and other tips to help her learn.

- Provide year-round children's reading and educational activities.

Simple Strategies for Creating Strong Readers

Without a doubt, reading with children spells success for early literacy. Putting a few simple strategies into action will make a significant difference in helping children develop into good readers and writers.

Through reading aloud, providing print materials, and promoting positive attitudes about reading and writing, you can have a powerful impact on children's literacy and learning.

- Invite a child to read with you every day.

- When reading a book where the print is large, point word by word as you read. This will help the child learn that reading goes from left to right and understand that the word he or she says is the word he or she sees.

- Read a child's favorite book over and over again.

- Read many stories with rhyming words and lines that repeat. Invite the child to join in on these parts. Point, word by word, as he or she reads along with you.

- Discuss new words. For example, "This big house is called a palace. Who do you think lives in a palace?"

- Stop and ask about the pictures and about what is happening in the story.

- Read from a variety of children's books, including fairy tales, song books, poems, and information books.

How Do I Know a Good Early Reading Program When I See One?

- Every teacher is excited about reading and promotes the value and fun of reading to students.

- All students are carefully evaluated, beginning in Kindergarten, to see what they know and what they need to become good readers.

- Reading instruction and practice lasts 90 minutes or more a day in first, second and third grades and 60 minutes a day in Kindergarten.

- All students in first, second and third grades who are behind in reading get special instruction and practice. They receive, throughout the day, a total of 60 extra minutes of instruction.

- Before or after-school help is given to all students beyond first grade who need extra instruction or who need to review skills. Summer school is available for students who are behind at the end of the year.

- Reading instruction and practice includes work on letters, sounds and blending sounds. Students learn to blend letters and sounds to form new words.

- Learning new words and their meaning is an important part of instruction.

- Students have daily spelling practice and weekly tests.

- The connection between reading and writing is taught on a daily basis. Students write daily. Papers are corrected and returned to the students. By the end of second grade, students write final copies of corrected papers. Corrected papers are sent home for parents to see.

- All students are read to each day from different kinds of books. Students discuss what they read with teachers and other students.

- All students have a chance to read both silently and aloud in school each day and at home every night.

- Every classroom has a library of books that children want to read. This includes easy books and books that are more difficult.

- The school library is used often and has many books. Students may check books out during the summer and over holidays.

The source of the information in this Chapter is a report published by the U.S. Department of Education, Office of Intergovernmental and Interagency Affairs, Educational Partnerships and Family Involvement Unit, Reading Tips for Parents, *Washington, DC, 2003. For more information see the* Resources and Bibliography *section of this book.*

A CHILD BECOMES A READER

Birth to Preschool

"Proven Ideas from Research for Parents"

When does a child learn to read? Many people might say, "In kindergarten or first grade." But researchers have told us something very important. Learning to read and write can start at home, long before children go to school. Children can start down the road to becoming readers from the day they are born.

Very early, children begin to learn about spoken language when they hear their family members talking, laughing, singing and when they respond to all of the sounds that fill their world. They begin to understand written language when they hear adults read stories to them and see adults reading newspapers, magazines and books for themselves. These early experiences with spoken and written language set the stage for children to become successful readers and writers.

This chapter gives you ideas for playing, talking, and reading with your child that will help him become a good reader and writer later in life. You don't need special training or expensive materials. For your baby or toddler, you can just include some simple, fun language games and activities into the things you already do together every day. For your preschooler, you can keep in touch with your child's teachers so that you know what he is learning in school and support that learning at home.

This Chapter Contains:

1. A short summary of what scientific research says about how children learn to read and write.

2. Things you can do with your children from birth through age 2 to help them become readers.

3. Things you can do with your children between the ages 3 and 4 to help them become readers.

4. What to look for in quality day care centers and preschools to help your children become readers.

5. A list of helpful terms (these appear in bold type throughout this chapter).

Remember, keep it simple and have fun. Make these activities part of the warm, loving relationship you are already creating with your child.

The Building Blocks of Reading and Writing

From several decades of research, we have learned a lot about how children learn to read and write. This research tells us that to become skilled and confident readers over time, young children need lots of opportunities to:

1. Build spoken language by talking and listening.

2. Learn about print and books.

3. Learn about the sounds of spoken language (this is called phonological awareness).

4. Learn about the letters of the alphabet.

5. Listen to books read aloud.

Talking and Listening

Remember the old saying "children should be seen and not heard?" Research tells us that for children to become readers, they should listen and talk a lot.

By the time children are one year old, they already know a lot about spoken language – talking and listening. They recognize some speech sounds. They know which sounds make the words that are important to them. They begin to imitate those sounds. Children learn all of this by listening to family members talk. Even "baby talk," which exaggerates the sounds and rhythms of words, makes a contribution to children's ability to understand language. Children who do not hear a lot of talk and who are not encouraged to talk themselves often have problems learning to read.

The information in this chapter comes from many research studies that examined early literacy development. The reports and books listed in the appendix offer more research-based information about how children learn to read and write.

Print and Books

Even though books don't come with operating instructions, we use them in certain ways. We hold them right-side up. We turn the pages one at a time. We read lines of words starting at the left and moving to the right. Knowing about print and books and how they are used is called print awareness.

Print awareness is an important part of knowing how to read and write. Children who know about print understand that the words they see in print and the words they speak and hear are related. They will use and see print a lot, even when they're young – on signs and billboards, in alphabet books and storybooks, and in labels, magazines, and newspapers. They see family members use print, and they learn that print is all around them and that it is used for different purposes.

Sounds in Spoken Language

Some words rhyme. Sentences are made up of separate words. Words have parts called syllables. The words bag, ball and bug all begin with the same sound. When a child begins to notice and understand these things about spoken language, he is developing phonological awareness – the ability to hear and work with the sounds of spoken language.

When a child also begins to understand that spoken

words are made up of separate, small sounds, he is developing phonemic awareness. These individual sounds in spoken language are called phonemes. For example, the word **big** has three phonemes, /**b**/ /**i**/ /**g**/.*

> * A letter between slash marks, /**b**/, shows the phoneme, or sound, that the letter represents, and not the name of the letter. For example, the letter **b** represents the sound /**b**/.

Children who have phonemic awareness can take spoken words apart, sound by sound (the name for this is segmentation) and put together sounds to make words (the name for this is blending). Research shows that how easily children learn to read can depend on how much phonological and phonemic awareness they have.

The ABCs

Singing the alphabet song is more than just a fun activity. Children who go to kindergarten already knowing the shapes and names of the letters of the alphabet, and how to write them, have an easier time learning to read. This is sometimes called alphabetic knowledge.

Reading Aloud

Reading aloud to children has been called the single most important activity for building the knowledge required for success in reading. Reading aloud, with children participating actively, helps children learn new words, learn more about the world, learn about written language and see the connection between spoken and written words.

Read Aloud Magic

Infants and Toddlers: Birth through Age 2

WHAT TO DO AT HOME

Talking to and reading to infants and toddlers are two good ways to prepare them for later success in reading.

Talk to Your Child

- Begin talking and singing to your child from birth. Your baby loves hearing your voice. Play peek-a-boo and pat-a-cake. Recite nursery rhymes or other verses that have strong rhythms and repeated sounds. Sing lullabies and other songs.

- Let your baby know that you hear her babbles, coos and gurgles. Repeat the sounds she makes. Smile back. When you respond to her sounds, she learns that what she "says" means something and is important to you. Sometimes, you can supply the language for her.

- Play simple touching and talking games. These help a child learn what different parts of the body are called.

- Point to familiar objects and name them. When a child hears an object called the same name over and over he learns to connect the spoken word with its meaning.

- When your child begins to speak, build his language. A child starts talking by using single words and short sentences. You can help by filling in missing words and using complete sentences.

- Encourage your child to talk with you. Ask questions that show you are interested in what she thinks and says. Ask her to share ideas and events that are important to her. Ask her questions that require her to talk, rather than just to give yes or no answers. Listen carefully to what she says.

- Listen to your child's questions and answer them patiently. Take time to explain things to him as completely as you can. Keep answering questions that your child asks again and again, because children learn from hearing things over and over.

Read to Your Child

- Make reading a pleasure. Read to your child in a comfortable place. Have her sit on your lap or next to you so that she can see and point to the print and the pictures. Show her that reading is fun and rewarding.

- Show enthusiasm as you read with your child. Read the story with expression. Make it more interesting by talking as the characters would talk, making sound effects and making expressions with your face and hands. When children enjoy being read to, they will grow to love books and be eager to learn to read them.

- Read to your child often. Set aside special times for reading each day, perhaps after lunch and at bedtime. The more you can read to him, the better—as long as he is willing to listen, and reading times can be brief. Just five to ten minutes is adequate when time is short.

- Talk with your child as you read together. Comment about what's happening in the story. Point to pictures and talk about what's happening in them. When your child is ready, have him tell you about the pictures.

- Encourage your child to explore books. Give your baby sturdy books to look at, touch, and hold. Allow her to turn the pages, look through the holes or lift the flaps. As your child grows older, keep books on low shelves or in baskets where she can see them and get them herself. Encourage her to look through the books and talk about them. She may talk about the pictures. She may "pretend" to read a book that she has heard many times. Or, she may pretend read based only on the pictures.

- Read favorite books again and again. Your child will probably ask you to read favorite books many times. You might get tired of reading the same books, but children love hearing the same stories again. And it helps them learn to read by hearing familiar words and seeing what they look like in print.

Reading Together

Even six-week-old babies like the feeling of closeness when a parent, grandparent or other caretaker reads to them. When children find out that reading with a loving adult can be a warm, happy experience, they begin to build a lifelong love of reading.

Reading aloud also helps children learn specific things about reading and words:

- About books – how to hold them. How to turn the pages one at a time. How books have words and pictures to help tell the story.

- About print – there is a difference between words and the pictures. You read words and look at pictures.

- About words – every word has a meaning. There are always new words to learn.

- About book language – sometimes book language sounds different from everyday conversation.

- About the world – there are objects, places, events and situations that they have not heard about before.

Good Books for Infants and Toddlers

- Board books are made from heavy cardboard with a plastic coating. The pages are easy for very young children to turn. Board books are sturdy and can stand hard wear by babies, who tend to throw them, crawl over them and chew them. Board books can be wiped clean.

- Cloth books, printed on fabric, are soft, strong and washable.

- Touch-and-feel books invite children to explore them with their fingers. They contain objects with different textures or contain holes or pages of different shapes.

- Interactive books have flaps that lift or other parts that move. Toddlers love them, but these books tend not to hold up well under rough treatment.

- Books with interesting language, rhythm and sounds such as books with rhymes, songs and poetry.

- Books with predictable patterns and repeated language such as traditional nursery rhymes or songs.

WHAT CHILDREN SHOULD BE DOING BY AGE 3

The following is a list of accomplishments that you can expect for your child by age 3. This list is based on research in the fields of reading, early childhood education and child development. Remember, though, that children don't develop and learn at the same pace and in the same way. Your child may be more advanced or need more help than others in her age group. You are, of course, the best judge of your child's abilities and needs. You should take the accomplishments as guidelines and not as hard-and-fast rules.

A Three-Year-Old Child:

- Likes reading with an adult on a regular basis.

- Listens to stories from books and stories that you tell.

- Recognizes a book by its cover.

- Pretends to read books.

- Understands that books are handled in certain ways.

- Looks at pictures in a book and knows they stand for real objects.

- Says the name of objects in books.

- Comments on characters in books.

- Asks an adult to read to him or to help him write.

- May begin paying attention to print such as letters in names.

- Begins to tell the difference between drawing and writing.

- Begins to scribble as a way of writing, making some forms that look like letters.

The main sources for this list of accomplishments are Preventing Reading Difficulties in Young Children *and* Learning to Read and Write: Developmentally Appropriate Practices for Young Children. *For more information about these sources, see the* Bibliography *at the end of this book.*

Preschoolers: Ages 3 and 4

At ages 3 and 4 children are growing rapidly in their language use and in their knowledge of reading and writing. They are learning the meanings of many new words, and they are beginning to use words in more complicated sentences when they speak. They know more about books and print. They are eager to write. They may even be showing an interest in learning to read.

Many three-year-old and four-year-old children attend day care centers or preschool for part or most of the day. The information in this section of the booklet will help you and your child, whether your child stays at home all day or attends a day care center or preschool.

WHAT TO DO AT HOME

Continue to talk and read with your child, as you did when he was an infant and toddler. Also, add some new and more challenging activities.

Talk and Listen

- When you do something together – talk about it (eating, shopping, taking a walk, visiting a relative, etc.).

- Take your child to new places and introduce him to new experiences. Talk about the new, interesting and unusual things that you see and do.

- Teach your child the meaning of new words. Say the names of things around the house. Label and talk about things in pictures. Explain, in simple ways, how to use familiar objects and how they work.

- Help your child to follow directions. Use short, clear sentences to tell him what you want him to do.

- Play with words. Have fun with tongue twisters such as "Peter Piper picked a peck of pickled peppers" and nonsense rhymes such as "Hey Diddle, Diddle," as well as more modern nonsense rhymes.

Read Together

- Keep reading to your child. Read her a lot of different kinds of books. Reread her favorite books, even if you get tired of them before she does.

- Read predictable books. Your child will begin to recognize the repeated words and phrases and have fun saying them with you.

- Read poetry and other rhyming books to your child. When reading a familiar rhyme, stop before a rhyming word and ask your child to provide the word.

- Ask your child what she thinks will happen next in a story. Get excited when she finds out whether her guess was right.

- Talk about books. Ask about favorite parts. Help your child relate the story to his own life. Answer his questions about characters or events.

- Build a library, or book collection, for your child. Look

for books at bookstores, garage sales, used bookstores and sales at the library. Suggest that people give books to your child as birthday gifts and on other special days.

Teach about Print and Letters

- Help your child learn to recognize her name in print. As she watches, print the letters of her name, saying each letter as you write it. Display her name in special places in your home. Encourage her to spell and write her name.

- Point out words and letters everywhere you can. Read street signs, traffic signs, billboards and store signs. Point out certain letters in these signs. Ask your child to begin naming common signs and find some letters.

- Teach your child the alphabet song.

- Share alphabet books with your child. Some alphabet books have songs and games that you can learn together.

- Put magnetic letters on your refrigerator or other smooth, safe metal surface. Ask your child to name the letters as he plays with them.

- Play games using the alphabet. Ask your child to find letters in books, magazines, newspapers and other print.

WHAT TO LOOK FOR IN DAY CARE CENTERS AND PRESCHOOLS

If your child attends a day care center or preschool, look for these important characteristics of teachers, classrooms and instruction.

Teachers

In quality day care centers and preschools, teachers:

- Keep a well-run, orderly classroom that also encourages children to participate in and enjoy learning.

- Use many creative ways to help children learn language and learn the knowledge and skills that will help them become readers.

Classrooms

In quality day care centers and preschools, classrooms have:

- Lots of books and magazines that children can handle and play with.

- Areas for many different activities, such as art, science, housekeeping, writing and perhaps computers.

- Plenty of print on labels, signs and posters.

- Writing materials (paper, pencils, crayons and markers).

- Magnetic letters or letters made of foam, plastic, wood or other durable material so children can pretend write and play.

Instruction

In quality day care centers and preschools teachers:

- Read aloud to children frequently, from many different kinds of books.

- Talk with children throughout the day and listen carefully to what they say.

- Play games such as "Simon Says" and "Mother, May I?" that require children to listen carefully.

- Give children opportunities to build their knowledge by exploring their interests and ideas.

- Help children learn the meanings of new words by naming colors, shapes, animals, familiar objects and parts of the classroom.

- Teach about the sounds of spoken language by reading aloud books with interesting sounds, chanting and rhyming; by having children say or sing nursery rhymes and songs; and by playing word games.

- Teach children about print by pointing out and using the print that is all around them.

- Teach the letters of the alphabet.

- Encourage children to scribble, draw and try to write.

<u>WHAT CHILDREN SHOULD BE DOING BY AGE 5</u>

The following is a list of some accomplishments that you can expect for your child by age 5. This list is based on research in the fields of reading, early childhood education, and child development. Remember, however, that children don't all develop and learn at the same pace and in the same way. Your child may be more advanced or need more help than others in her age group. You are, of course, the best judge of your child's abilities and needs. You should take the accomplishments as guidelines and not as hard-and-fast rules.

Spoken Language

A five-year-old child:

- Understands and follows oral (or spoken) directions.

- Uses new words and longer sentences when she speaks.

- Recognizes the beginning sounds of words and sounds that rhyme.

- Listens carefully when books are read aloud.

Reading

A five-year-old child:

- Shows interest in books and reading.

- Might try to read, calling attention to himself and showing pride in what he can do ("See, I can read this book!").

- Can follow the series of events in some stories.

- Can connect what happens in books to her life and experiences.

- Asks questions and makes comments that show he understands the book he is listening to.

Print and Letters

A five-year-old child:

- Knows the difference between print (words) and pictures and knows that print is what you read.

- Recognizes print around him on signs, on television, on boxes, and many other places.

- Understands that writing has a lot of different purposes. For example, signs tell where something is located, lists can be used for grocery shopping, directions can tell you how to put something together.

- Knows that each letter in the alphabet has a name.

- Can name at least ten letters in the alphabet, especially the letters in her name.

- "Writes" or scribbles messages.

The main sources for this list of accomplishments are Preventing Reading Difficulties in Young Children *and* Learning to Read and Write: Developmentally Appropriate Practices for Young Children. *For more information about these sources, see the* Bibliography *at the end of this book.*

Some Helpful Terms to Know (Basic)

Day care providers and preschool teachers might use some of the following terms when talking to you about how your child is learning to read. You will find that many of these terms are used in this book.

alphabetic knowledge – Knowing the names and shapes of the letters of the alphabet.

big books – Oversized books that allow for the sharing of print and illustrations with children.

blending – Putting together individual sounds to make spoken words.

developmental spelling – The use of letter-sound relationship information to attempt to write words.

emergent literacy – The view that literacy learning begins at birth and is encouraged through participation with adults in meaningful reading and writing activities.

environmental print – Print that is a part of everyday life, such as signs, billboards, labels and business logos.

experimental writing – Efforts by young children to experiment with writing by creating pretend and real letters and by organizing scribbles and marks on paper.

invented spelling – See developmental spelling.

literacy – Includes all the activities involved in speaking, listening, reading, writing and appreciating both spoken and written language.

phonemes – The smallest parts of spoken language that combine to form words. For example, the word *hit* is made up of three phonemes (/**h**/ /**i**/ /**t**/) and differs by one phoneme from the words *pit*, *hip* and *hot*.

phonemic awareness – The ability to notice and work with the individual sounds in spoken language.

phonological awareness – The understanding that spoken language is made up of individual and separate sounds. In addition to phonemes, phonological awareness activities can involve work with rhymes, words, sentences and syllables.

pretend reading – Children's attempts to "read" a book before they have learned to read. Usually children pretend read familiar books that they have practically memorized.

print awareness – Knowing about print and books and how they are used.

segmentation – Taking spoken words apart sound by sound.

spoken language – The language used in talking and listening; in contrast to written language, which is the language used in writing and reading.

syllable – A word part that contains a vowel or, in spoken language, a vowel sound (*e-vent*, *news-pa-per*, *pret-ty*).

vocabulary – The words we must know in order to communicate effectively. *Oral* vocabulary refers to words that we use in speaking or recognize in listening.

The source of the information in this Chapter is a report published by the U.S. Government, National Institute for Literacy and The Partnership for Reading, A Child Becomes a Reader – Proven Ideas from Research: Birth through Preschool (Third Edition, 2006)*, Jessup, MD.*

A CHILD BECOMES A READER

Kindergarten to Grade 3

"Proven Ideas from Research for Parents"

The road to becoming a reader begins the day a child is born and continues through the end of third grade. At that point, a child must read with ease and understanding to take advantage of the learning opportunities in fourth grade and beyond – in school and in life.

Learning to read and write starts at home, long before children go to school. Very early, children begin to learn about the sounds of spoken language when they hear their family members talking, laughing and singing, and when they respond to all of the sounds that fill their world. They begin to understand written language when they hear adults read stories to them and see adults reading newspapers, magazines and books for themselves.

Your role in setting your child on the road to becoming a successful reader and writer does not end when she begins kindergarten.

This Chapter Contains:

1. A short summary of what scientific research says about how children learn to read and write.

2. Things you can do with your children at various grade levels (kindergarten to third grade) to help them become readers.

3. What to look for in quality reading instruction at each grade level.

4. A list of helpful terms (these appear in bold type throughout this chapter).

Try a few activities from this chapter with your child. You don't need special training or expensive materials. Just include the activities in the things you already do together every day. Make these activities part of the warm, loving relationship you are continuing to build with your child.

The main source of information in this Chapter is the report of the National Reading Panel, Teaching Children to Read: An Evidence-Based Assessment of the Scientific Research Literature on Reading and Its Implications for Reading Instruction. *This report, along with the other reports and books listed at the back of this book, offers more research-based information about how children learn to read and write.*

The Building Blocks of Reading and Writing

From several decades of research we have learned a lot about how children learn to read and write. This research tells us that to become more skilled and confident readers over time children need lots of opportunities to:

1. Build spoken language by talking and listening.

2. Learn about print and books.

3. Learn about the sounds of spoken language (this is called phonological awareness).

4. Learn about the letters of the alphabet.

5. Be read to and read on their own.

6. Learn and use letter-sound relationships (this is called phonics) and be able to recognize words when they see them.

7. Spell and write.

8. Develop their ability to read quickly and naturally (this is called fluency).

9. Learn new words and build their knowledge of what words mean (this is called vocabulary).

10. Build their knowledge of the world.

11. Build their ability to understand what they read (this is called comprehension).

Talking and Listening

Remember the old saying "children should be seen and not heard"? Research tells us that for children to become readers they should listen and talk a lot.

By the time children are one year old they already know a lot about spoken language – talking and listening. They recognize some speech sounds. They know which sounds make the words that are important to them. They begin to imitate those sounds. Children learn all of this by listening to family members talk. Even "baby talk," which exaggerates the sounds and rhythms of words, makes a contribution to children's ability to understand language. Children who do not hear a lot of talk and who are not encouraged to talk themselves often have problems learning to read.

Print and Books

Even though books don't come with operating instructions, we use them in certain ways. We hold books right-side up. We turn the pages one at a time. We read lines of words starting at the left and moving to the right. Knowing about print and books and how they are used is called print awareness.

Print awareness is an important part of knowing how to read and write. Children who know about print understand that the words they see in print and the words they speak and hear are related. They will use and see print a lot, even when they're young, on signs and billboards, in alphabet books and storybooks, and in labels, magazines and newspapers. They see family members use print, and they learn that print is all around them and that it is used for different purposes.

Sounds in Spoken Language

Some words rhyme. Sentences are made up of separate words. Words have parts called syllables. The words bag, ball and bug all begin with the same sound. When a child begins to notice and understand these things, he is developing phonological awareness – the ability to hear and work with the sounds of spoken language.

When a child also begins to understand that spoken words are made up of separate, small sounds, he is developing phonemic awareness. These individual sounds in spoken language are called phonemes. For example, the word big has three phonemes: /**b**/ /**i**/ /**g**/.*

---

* A letter between slash marks, /**b**/, shows the phoneme, or sound, that the letter represents and not the name of the letter. For example, the letter **b** represents the sound /**b**/.

Children who have phonemic awareness can take spoken words apart sound by sound (the name for this is segmentation) and put together sounds to make words (the name for this is blending). Research shows that how easily children learn to read can depend on how much phonological and phonemic awareness they have.

The ABCs

Singing the alphabet song is more than just a fun activity. Children who go to kindergarten already knowing the shapes and names of the letters of the alphabet, and how to write them, have a much easier time learning to read. Knowing the names and shapes of letters is sometimes called alphabetic knowledge.

Reading Aloud

Reading aloud to children has been called the single most important activity for building the knowledge required for success in reading.

Reading aloud, with children participating actively, helps children learn new words, learn more about the world, learn about written language, and see the connection between words that are spoken and words that are written.

Phonics and Word-Study Skills

Phonics instruction helps beginning readers see the relationships between the sounds of spoken language and the letters of written language. Understanding these relationships gives children a tool that they can use to recognize familiar words quickly and to figure out new words.

Word-study instruction is the step that follows phonics instruction. It helps older children learn to apply their phonics knowledge and knowledge of word parts (such as prefixes, suffixes and root words) as they read and write words. Rapid word recognition means that children spend less time struggling over words and have more time getting meaning from what they read, which, of course, is the real purpose for reading.

Spelling and Writing

Children learn more about how print works when they spell and write on their own. When they begin to write, children draw and scribble. Later, they use what they are learning about sounds and letters when they try to write words. This often is called invented, or developmental, spelling. Because invented spelling encourages children to think about the sounds in words and how the sounds are related to letters, it can help preschool and kindergarten children develop both as readers and writers. However, after kindergarten, children need well-organized, systematic lessons in spelling to help them become good spellers.

Fluency

Fluency is the word for being able to read quickly and accurately. Fluent readers recognize words automatically. They are able to group words quickly to help them get the meaning of what they read. When fluent readers read aloud, they read smoothly and with expression. Their reading sounds natural, like speech. Readers who have not yet developed fluency read slowly, word by word. Sometimes, their oral reading is choppy and plodding. They may make a lot of mistakes.

Most beginning readers do not read fluently. However, by the end of first grade children should be reading their grade level books fluently.

Vocabulary and Knowledge of the World

Vocabulary is the name for words we must know in order to listen, speak, read and write effectively. Time and again researchers have found strong connections between the size of children's vocabularies, how well they comprehend what they read, and how well they do in school.

Children who are poor readers often do not have the vocabulary knowledge they need to get meaning from what they read. Because reading is difficult for them they cannot and do not read very much. As a result, they may not see new words in print often enough to learn them. Good readers read more, become better readers and learn more words; poor readers read less, become poorer readers and learn fewer words.

Children learn vocabulary in two ways: *indirectly*, by hearing and seeing words as they listen, talk, and read; and *directly* by parents and teachers teaching them the meanings of certain words.

Vocabulary and knowledge of the world are, of course, very closely tied together. Children who know something about the world are much better able to understand what they read about in school.

Comprehension

Comprehension means getting meaning from what we read. It is the heart of reading. Research shows that knowledge of letter-sound relationships and comprehension go hand-in-hand. If children can sound out the words but don't understand what they are reading, they're not really reading.

Children can build their comprehension by learning to use mental plans, or strategies, to get meaning as they read.

These strategies include using what they already know to make sense of what they read, making predictions, paying attention to the way a reading selection is organized, creating mental pictures, asking questions and summarizing.

Kindergarten

WHAT TO DO AT HOME

Talk Often with Your Child to Build Listening and Talking Skills

- Talk with your child often as you eat together, shop for groceries, walk to school, wait for a bus and many other occasions. As she gets ready for school, ask about the stories and poems she is reading and what projects she has in science or art time. Ask about friends and classmates (encourage her to use their names) and to describe the games they like to play together. Ask questions that will encourage her to talk, and not just give "yes" or "no " answers.

- Have your child use his imagination to make up and tell you stories. Ask questions that will encourage him to expand the stories.

- Have a conversation about recent family photographs. Ask your child to describe each picture: who is in it, what's happening, and where the picture was taken.

- Listen to your child's questions patiently and answer them just as patiently. If you don't know the answer to a question, you can work together to find one (look things up in a book or on the computer, for example).

- Talk about books that you've read together. Ask your child about favorite parts and characters and answer his questions about events or characters.

- Pay attention to how much TV your child is watching. Set aside "no TV" time each day and use that time to talk together.

- Tell stories about your childhood. Make a story out of something that happened, such as a special birthday or a visit to a zoo or city.

Show Your Child How Books and Print Work

- As you read with your child, have him point out such things as front and back covers and the title. Have him point out the names of authors and illustrators and tell what those people do. Have him show you where you should start reading on a page.

- Help your child make connections between print and pictures as you read. Have him find details in the pictures, then help her find and point to the words that name those details.

Focus Your Child's Attention on the Sounds of Spoken Language

- Sing or say nursery rhymes and songs.

- Play word games.

- Read a story or poem and ask your child to listen for words that begin with the same sound. Have her say the words. Then have her say another word that begins with that sound.

- As you read, stop and say a simple word. Have your child say the sounds in the word, write the letters for the sounds and then read what she wrote.

Have Your Child Identify and Name the Letters of the Alphabet

- Point out letters and have your child name them.

- Make an alphabet book with your child. Have her draw pictures or cut pictures from magazines or use old photos. Paste each picture into the book. With your child, write the first letter of the word that stands for the object or person in the picture (for example, B for bird, M for milk, and so forth).

Support What Your Child is Learning in School about the Relationship between Letters and Sounds

- Point out labels, boxes, newspapers, magazines and signs that display words with letter-sound relationships that your child is learning in kindergarten.

- Listen to your child read words and books from school. Be patient and listen as your child practices. Let your child know you are proud of what he is learning.

Encourage Your Child to Spell and Write

- When your child is writing, encourage her to spell words using what she knows about sounds and letters.

- Encourage your child to write notes, e-mails and letters to family members and friends. You may have your child tell you the message for you to write to include with her original work.

- Have your child create his own picture book made with his own drawings or with pictures that he cuts from magazines. Help him to label the pictures. Include pictures that illustrate the new words he is learning.

Help Your Child Build Vocabulary, Knowledge of the World and Comprehension

- As you read aloud, pause from time to time to ask him about the meaning of the book. Help him make connections between his life and what's happening in the book. Explain new ideas and words to him. Encourage your child to ask questions about the book. Ask him to retell the story or to tell in his own words what the book was about.

- Use and repeat important words such as names of buildings, parks, zoos, cities and other places you visit.

- Help your child develop an interest in the world. Read to her from your magazines and newspapers, as well as from informational (nonfiction) children's books. Help her to explore ideas and interests by using appropriate web sites.

WHAT TO LOOK FOR IN KINDERGARTEN CLASSROOMS

In effective kindergarten classrooms you will see literacy instruction that focuses on:

Developing Talking and Listening Abilities

The teacher shows children appropriate ways to talk and listen, ask and answer questions, and give and follow directions.

The children talk with teachers and classmates about what they have read and heard. They retell stories that they have heard read aloud. They make up and tell their own stories. They may pretend to be characters in play centers.

Teaching about Books and Print

The teacher shows children how books should be handled, how they are read from front to back, from the top to the bottom of a page, and from left to right on a page. He talks about the various kinds of print in the classroom, including their meaning and purpose.

The children enjoy books and reading. They see lots of print around them being used in many ways. They are curious about the print and eager to learn what it means.

Teaching about the Alphabet

The teacher helps children learn the names and shapes of all the letters of the alphabet and encourages the children to play with letters and to write using letters.

The children listen to the teacher read them an alphabet book, then sing the alphabet song. Some children play with plastic letters, while others say the letters as they write their own names.

Teaching the Sounds of Spoken Language

The teacher provides explicit instruction in phonological awareness and phonemic awareness. The teacher has children put together sounds (blending) to make words and break words into separate sounds (segmentation). As the children write, he promotes phonemic awareness by encouraging them to use what they know about the sounds that make up words.

The children have fun with the sounds of words. Early in the year, they tell which words in a story rhyme; they may make up their own nonsense rhymes. A little later in the year, they listen for the beginning sounds of the words in a poem. They also may clap out the number of syllables in their names and in words. Late in the year, they put together and take apart the separate sounds in words. They begin to relate sounds to letters and to write the letters for the sounds that they hear.

Phonemic Awareness

What blending and segmentation look like:

Phoneme <u>blending</u>:

Teachers say a word phoneme by phoneme, then have the children repeat the sequence of phonemes and combine the phonemes to say the word.

Continued...

> **Teacher:** /s/ /u/ /n/
>
> **Children:** /s/ /u/ /n/; **sun.**
>
> **Phoneme <u>segmentation</u>:**
>
> Teachers say a word, then have the children break it into its separate phonemes, saying each one as they tap out or count it.
>
> **Teacher: Slim**
>
> **Children:** /s/ /l/ /i/ /m/.
>
> **Teacher:** How many sounds are in **slim**?
>
> **Children:** Four sounds.
>
> A letter between slash marks, /**b**/, shows the phoneme, or sound, that the letter represents, and not the name of the letter. For example, the letter **b** represents the sound /b/.

Teaching Phonics

The teacher uses explicit instruction to teach children a set of the most useful letter-sound relationships.

The children read easy books containing words with letter-sound relationships they are learning. They are also writing the relationships they know in words, sentences, messages and their own stories.

Developing Spelling and Writing

The teacher has children practice their new writing

skills in groups with other children and at learning centers. She makes spelling development a part of writing activities.

The children, depending on the time of the year, scribble, draw, label pictures and use their growing knowledge of sounds and letters to write messages. They are becoming aware of correct spellings for some words, especially their names.

Building Vocabulary and Knowledge of the World

The teacher talks with the children about important new words and ideas as she reads aloud. She helps them connect the new words to their own knowledge and experiences. She discusses words that are most important for understanding the reading selection. She emphasizes words that the children are likely to see and use often and she teaches the meaning of new words over an extended period of time. She thinks about the content of the books that she reads to the children and chooses books that build on and expand the children's knowledge.

The children learn lots of new words and like to share their new words with their families. They see the teacher's enthusiasm for words and enjoy playing with words and language. They use words that are important to their schoolwork, such as the names for colors, shapes and numbers. They explore new ideas and learn new words.

Building Comprehension

The teacher reads aloud to children often and discusses books before, during and after reading. She reads many different kinds of books, including "make-believe" (fiction), "real" (nonfiction) and poetry. She shows children how good readers get meaning from what they read.

The children listen to and understand what is read to them. They answer the teacher's questions. They make connections between what they already know and what they are reading about. They talk about what they learned from nonfiction books they have read and they retell or act out important events in stories. They identify the characters, settings and events in stories.

WHAT CHILDREN SHOULD BE ABLE TO DO BY THE END OF KINDERGARTEN

The following is a list of some accomplishments that you can expect of your child by the end of kindergarten. This list is based on research in the fields of reading, early childhood education and child development. Remember, though, that children don't develop and learn at the same pace and in the same way. Your child may be more advanced or need more help than others in her age group. You are, of course, the best judge of your child's abilities and needs. You should view these accomplishments as guidelines and not as hard-and-fast rules. If you have concerns about your child's reading development, talk to his teacher.

Books and Print

By the end of kindergarten a child:

- Knows the parts of a book and how books are held and read.

- Identifies a book's title and understands what authors and illustrators do.

- Follows print from left to right and from top to bottom of a page when stories are read aloud.

- Understands the relationship between print and pictures.

- Understands that the message of most books is in the print and not the pictures.

The Alphabet

By the end of kindergarten a child:

- Recognizes the shapes and names of all the letters in the alphabet (both uppercase and lowercase letters).

- Writes many uppercase and lowercase letters on his own.

Sounds in Spoken Language

By the end of kindergarten a child:

- Understands that spoken words are made up of separate sounds.

- Recognizes and makes rhymes.

- Identifies words that have the same beginning sound.

- Puts together, or blends, spoken sounds into simple words.

Phonics and Word Recognition

By the end of kindergarten a child:

- Knows a number of letter-sound relationships.

- Understands that the order of letters in a written word represents the order of sounds in a spoken word.

- Recognizes some common words on sight, such as *a, the, I, said, you, is and are.*

Reading

By the end of kindergarten a child:

- Listens carefully to books read aloud.

- Asks and answers questions about stories.

- Uses what he already knows to help him understand a story.

- Predicts what will happen in a story based on pictures or information in the story.

- Retells and/or acts out stories.

- Knows the difference between "made-up" (fiction) and "real" (nonfiction) books and the difference between stories and poems.

Spelling and Writing

By the end of kindergarten a child:

- Uses phonemic awareness and letter knowledge to spell and write words.

- Begins to spell some words correctly.

- Writes his own first and last name and the first names

of some friends, classmates or family members.

- Writes some letters and words as they are said to her.

Vocabulary and Knowledge of the World

By the end of kindergarten a child:

- Plays with and is curious about words and language.

- Uses new words in her own speech.

- Knows and uses words that are important to school work, such as the names for colors, shapes and numbers.

- Knows and uses words that are important to daily life, such as street names, addresses and names for community workers.

The main sources for this list of accomplishments are Preventing Reading Difficulties in Young Children. *For more information about this book, see the* Bibliography *at the end of this book.*

First Grade

WHAT TO DO AT HOME

The Top Three

1. Talk with your child to build listening and talking skills.

2. Read to and with your child – often. Talk to him about the words and ideas in books.

3. Ask your child's teacher how you can help your child practice at home what he is learning at school.

If your child needs help with developing phonemic awareness or identifying and naming letters of the alphabet, read the suggestions in the kindergarten section of this book. Remember that these two skills are very important in helping children learn to read and write.

Support What Your Child is Learning in School about Relationships between Letters and Sounds

- Listen to your child read books from school. Be patient as he practices. Let him know you're proud of his reading.

- Say the sounds of letters and ask your child to write the letter or letters that represent the sound.

- Ask your child to point out letter-sound relationships he's learning in the things you're reading together (books, calendars, labels, magazines, newspapers, etc.).

- Play word games. On cards, write words that contain the letter-sound relationships he is learning at school. Take turns choosing a card and blending the sounds to make the word. Then use the word in a sentence.

Encourage Your Child to Spell and Write

- Say a word your child knows and have him repeat the word. Then help him write the word the way he hears it.

- Write a word on paper and cut the letters apart (or use plastic or foam letters). Mix the letters and have your child spell a word by putting the letters in order.

- As you are reading with your child, point out words that have similar spellings, such as hop and pop. Ask him to write similar words, for example, top, mop and cop.

- Encourage your child to write often – for example, letters, thank-you notes, simple stories and grocery lists.

Help Your Child Build Vocabulary, Knowledge of the World and Comprehension

- When you read together, stop now and then to talk about the meaning of the book. Help her make connections between what's happening in the book and her life and experiences, or to other books you've read together. Ask her questions so that she talks about the information in a nonfiction book or about the characters or events of a fiction book. Encourage your child to ask questions. Ask her to explain what the book was about, in her own words.

- Before you come to the end of a story, ask your child to predict what might happen next or how the story will end.

- Talk about new words and ideas that your child has read or heard. Ask her to make up sentences with the new words or use the words in other situations. Help her to find out more about new ideas by using appropriate web sites.

- Read magazines and newspapers together. Get him interested in what's happening in other parts of the world.

WHAT TO LOOK FOR IN FIRST GRADE CLASSROOMS

In effective first grade classrooms you will see literacy instruction that focuses on:

Developing Talking and Listening Abilities

The teacher helps children use language that is appropriate for different audiences and purposes.

The children use speaking and listening for many purposes, including getting and giving information, giving opinions and talking with teachers and classmates. They talk about what has been read to them or what they have read. They retell stores that they have heard read aloud. They make up and tell stories based on their own experiences. They use the more formal language expected at school, such as complete sentences.

Teaching about Books and Print

The teacher reads aloud to the children often, sharing many different types of books and other print materials. She shows her enthusiasm for reading and her eagerness for the children to learn to read. As she reads, she shows the parts of print such as the beginnings and endings of sentences, new paragraphs and different punctuation marks.

The children are excited about being read to and about learning to read. They recognize the titles of books and ask the teacher to read their favorites. They spend part of the day looking at books or *pretend reading* books of their choice.

Teaching about the Alphabet

The teacher makes sure that children can recognize and name all of the letters of the alphabet, both uppercase and lowercase.

The children can quickly name the letters of the alphabet in order and recognize all letters. They use their knowledge of letters when they write.

Teaching Phonemic Awareness

The teacher provides explicit instruction in phonemic awareness. She shows the children how to do phonemic awareness activities and helps them with feedback. The activities are short and fun.

The children practice a lot with phonemes. For example, they clap out the sounds they hear in words (segmentation), put sounds together to make words (blending), add or drop sounds from words (phoneme addition and deletion), and replace sounds in words (phoneme substitution).

Phonemic Awareness

Awareness activities that you may see in first grade classrooms:

Phoneme deletion: Children recognize the word that remains when you take away a phoneme.

Teacher: What is **space** without the /**s**/?

Children: space without the /**s**/ is **pace**.

Phoneme addition: Children make a new word by adding a phoneme to a word.

Teacher: What word do you have if you add /**p**/ to the beginning of **lace**?

Children: Place.

Phoneme substitution: Children substitute one phoneme for another to make a new word.

Teacher: The word is **rag**. Change /**g**/ to /**n**/. What's the new word?

Children: Ran.

Teaching Phonics and Word Recognition

The teacher explicitly teaches the children letter-sound relationships in a clear and useful sequence. The teacher also teaches children irregular words they will see and read often but do not follow the letter-sound relationships they are learning. These are often called sight words (words such as *said, is, was* and *are).*

The children learn to blend sounds to read words – first, simple one-syllable words and later, words with more than one syllable. They read easy books that include the letter-sound relationships they are learning as well as sight words that they have been taught. They recognize and figure out the meaning of compound words (words made of two words put together, such as background). They practice writing the letter-sound relationships in words, sentences, messages and their own stories.

Phonemic Instruction

Although there are several different approaches to teaching phonics, here are some activities that you are likely to see in first grade classrooms.

- Children sort out objects and pictures by the beginning sounds they have studied such as /b/, /c/ and /t/. They put the objects in baskets labeled with the beginning letter. "I have a turtle. It goes in the T basket." "This cup goes in the C basket."

- The teacher teaches the -ing spelling pattern and sounds, pointing out -ing words in books. The children look for examples of -ing words in books in the classroom library. "I found singing!" "This book has a wing!" They copy the words on index cards and add them to the word wall under the heading "-ing words."

- The teacher helps children use plastic letters to spell out words containing sounds they have studied. She starts with two letter words and moves on to longer words. "Find two letters and make the word 'in'. Now add one letter to make the word pin. Now add a letter to make the word spin. Using those same letters, change the word to pins."

- The teacher reads a poem written on chart paper to the class, pointing to each word as he reads. When he's done, he invites children to circle the words beginning with the /p/ sound, saying the word as they circle it.

Developing Spelling and Writing

The teacher provides opportunities for children to practice writing skills independently in both whole group and learning center settings. She makes spelling a part of writing activities. She helps children begin to think through their writing efforts – planning, writing drafts and revising.

The children use writing more and more as a way to communicate ideas. They begin to organize their writing by planning, writing a draft copy and editing it. They continue to use some invented spelling, but are learning the correct spellings of most of the words that they write.

Building Vocabulary and Knowledge of the World

The teacher talks with the children about important new vocabulary words and helps them relate the new words to their own knowledge and experience. He makes a point of using new words in classroom discussions. He urges the children to use these words when they talk and write.

The children talk about the meanings of words and use new words when they talk and write. They begin to recognize words that are alike (synonyms) and words that are opposite (antonyms). They also begin to recognize the roles of different words in sentences – words that name (nouns) and words that show action (verbs). They understand that the language they use in school is more formal than the language they use at home and with friends.

Building Comprehension

The teacher reads aloud to children often and discusses books with them before, during and after reading. The teacher listens to children read aloud, corrects their errors and asks them questions about what they are reading. He shows children how to use mental plans or strategies to get meaning from what they read.

The children read aloud with accuracy and show that they understand what they're reading. They read books (fiction, nonfiction and poetry) that are appropriate for the time in the school year. They make connections between what they already know and what they are reading. They pay attention to their reading and recognize when something doesn't make sense.

They summarize and discuss what they read with classmates and their teacher. They choose to read on their own and enjoy reading.

WHAT CHILDREN SHOULD BE ABLE TO DO BY THE END OF FIRST GRADE

The following is a list of some accomplishments you can expect of your child by the end of first grade. This list is based on research in the fields of reading, early childhood education and child development. Remember, though, that children don't develop and learn at the same pace and in the same way. Your child may be more advanced or need more help than others in her age group. You are, of course, the best judge of your child's abilities and needs. You should take the accomplishments as guidelines and not as hard-and-fast rules. If you have concerns or questions about your child's reading development, talk to his teacher.

Books and Print

By the end of first grade a child:

- Knows the difference between letters and words.

- Knows that there are spaces between words in print.

- Knows that print represents spoken language and contains meaning.

- Knows some of the parts of print, such as the beginnings and endings of sentences, where paragraphs begin and end, and different punctuation marks.

- Understands why people read – to learn and enjoy.

The Alphabet

By the end of first grade a child:

- Can recognize and name all letters of the alphabet.

Sounds in Spoken Language

By the end of first grade a child:

- Can count the number of syllables in a word.

- Can put together and break apart the sounds of most single syllable words.

Phonics and Word Recognition

By the end of first grade a child:

- Can show how spoken words are represented by written letters that are arranged in a specific order.

- Can read one-syllable words using what he knows about phonics.

- Uses phonics to sound out words he doesn't know.

- Can recognize some irregularly spelled words, such as have, said, you and are.

Reading

By the end of first grade a child:

- Reads aloud first grade books and understands what they mean.

- Can tell when he is having problems understanding what he is reading.

- Reads and understands simple written instructions.

- Predicts what will happen next in a story.

- Discusses what she already knows about topics of books she is reading.

- Can ask questions (how, why, what if?) about books she is reading.

- Can describe, in his own words, what he has learned from a book he is reading.

- Can give a reason for why he is reading a book. (For example, to be entertained, to follow directions or learn about a nonfiction topic.)

Spelling and Writing

By the end of first grade a child:

- Uses invented (or developmental) spelling to try to spell words on his own.

- Understands that there is a correct way to spell words.

- Uses simple punctuation marks and capital letters.

- Writes for different purposes – stories, explanations, letters, lists, etc.

- Writes things for others to read (by thinking of ideas, writing draft copies and revising drafts).

Vocabulary and Knowledge of the World

By the end of first grade, a child:

- Uses language with more control (such as speaking in complete sentences).

- Understands that the language used in school is more formal than the language used at home and with friends.

- Talks about the meaning of words and uses new words when he speaks and writes.

- Begins to see that some words mean the same thing (synonyms) and some words have opposite meanings (antonyms).

- Begins to recognize that words play different roles in sentences. For example, some words (nouns) name things and some words (verbs) show action.

The main source for the list of accomplishments is Preventing Reading Difficulties in Young Children. *For more information about this book, see the* Bibliography *in the back of this book.*

Second and Third Grades

WHAT TO DO AT HOME

The Top Three

1. Talk often with your child to build listening and speaking skills.

2. Read to and with your child – often. Talk to her about the words and ideas in books. Encourage her to read on her own.

3. Ask your child's teacher how you can help your child practice at home what she is learning at school.

Use Reading Opportunities to Help Your Child Develop Fluency

- Listen to your child read books that he has brought home from school. Be patient as your child practices reading. Let him know that you are proud of his reading.

- If your child is not a very fluent reader (that is, she reads slowly and makes lots of mistakes), ask her to reread a paragraph or page a few times.

Find Opportunities for Your Child to Spell and Write

- Encourage your child to write often – for example, letters and thank-you notes to relatives and friends, simple stories, e-mails and items for the grocery list.

- Help your child learn the correct spellings of words.

Find Opportunities to Help Your Child Develop Vocabulary, Knowledge of the World, and Comprehension

- Talk about new words that your child has read or heard. Ask her to make up sentences with the new words.

- Help your child use the dictionary or thesaurus to check on the meanings of new words she reads or hears.

- Help your child become aware of prefixes, suffixes and root words. Point them out in books you are reading together or in print materials around the house. Ask her to think of other words related to the words you are discussing.

- Show your child how to use context – the sentences, words and pictures around an unfamiliar word – to figure out the word's meaning.

- As you read a book with your child, stop now and then to talk to her about the meaning of the book. Help her relate the experiences or events in the book to experiences or events in her life or to other books you have read together. Ask her questions that encourage her to talk about the information in a nonfiction book or about the characters or events of a fiction book. Encourage your child to ask questions. Ask her to tell in her own words what the book was about.

WHAT TO LOOK FOR IN SECOND AND THIRD GRADE CLASSROOMS

In effective second and third grade classrooms you will see literacy instruction that focuses on:

Promoting Reading Accuracy

The teacher helps children continue to use their knowledge of phonics to sound out and pronounce new words. The teacher helps children recognize simple, common spelling patterns in words. She also helps children learn the spellings and meanings of word parts such as prefixes, suffixes and root words.

The children become more able to read words accurately by using their knowledge of phonics. They use the other words in a sentence (the context) to figure out the pronunciations and meanings of new words.

Building Fluency

The teacher reads aloud to children, modeling fluent reading. She makes sure that children are working on developing fluency and monitors their progress. By listening to children read aloud, or by timing children's reading rates, the teacher ensures that children are becoming fluent readers.

The children are becoming more fluent readers by reading, reading, reading. They are improving their oral reading fluency by reading selections aloud.

Fluency Instruction

In second and third grade classrooms, effective

instruction will include some of the following activities for building fluency:

- Teachers listen to individual children read aloud and provide assistance and encouragement as they repeatedly read until they are fluent.

- Teachers read aloud and children read along as a group. The children repeat the reading until they are fluent.

- In a listening center, children read along in their books as they listen to a fluent reader read a book on an audiotape. The children read with the tape until they can read the book without support.

- Pairs of children read paragraphs from a book to each other, taking turns and assisting each other until they can read the paragraphs fluently.

- Teachers time children as they read aloud paragraphs or pages of a selection. They also note children's reading errors.

Teaching Spelling and Writing

The teacher teaches some common spelling patterns. He encourages children to write in many different forms, such as letters, stories, poetry, reviews, directions and reports. He helps children prepare for and plan their writing. He teaches them how to revise, edit and refine what they have written and helps them write using a computer.

The children write often, and for different audiences and purposes. They correctly spell previously studied words.

When they spell new words, they represent all of the sounds in the words. In their writing, the children use figurative language, dialogue and vivid descriptions. They read their writing to others and discuss one another's writing, offering helpful suggestions.

Developing Vocabulary and Knowledge of the World

The teacher is excited about words and shows students that they have a personal interest in learning new and intriguing words. He tries to develop children's awareness of and interest in words, their meanings and their power. As the teacher reads aloud to children, he discusses some of the important new words in the book. He relates new words to words the children already know and to their experiences. The teacher encourages children to read a lot, both in school and outside of school. He encourages them to explore topics that interest them and to use a variety of sources of information, including the Internet.

The children are interested in learning new words and are eager to share new vocabulary at school and at home. They are learning how to figure out the meanings of unknown words by using word parts such as prefixes, suffixes and root words. They can use different parts of speech correctly, including nouns, verbs, adjectives and adverbs. They read a lot on their own, and explore topics independently, often using computers.

Vocabulary Instruction

In second and third grade classrooms, effective instruction will include both specific word instruction and instruction in word learning strategies.

Specific word instruction:

- Teachers teach specific words from selections the students are about to read. These words are important for the students to know in order to understand what they will read.

- Teachers use new words for an extended period of time.

- The children see, hear and work with the words in many ways and in various contexts.

Word learning strategies:

- Teachers show children how to use the dictionary and thesaurus to learn about the meanings of words. Teachers show how some words have more than one definition, and they teach children how to find the right definition for their particular situation.

- Teachers teach children how to use word parts (prefixes, suffixes and root words) to determine the meaning of unknown words.

- Teachers provide instruction in how to use the meanings of known words in a reading selection (context) to figure out the meaning of unknown words.

Increasing Comprehension

The teacher guides children's understanding of what they are reading by discussing selections with them before, during and after reading. The teacher shows children how to use simple strategies to get meaning from what they read.

The children read many different kinds of books, both with the teacher's guidance and on their own. They offer answers to *"how," "why,"* and *"what-if"* questions, and read to find the answers to their own questions. They compare and contrast characters and events across stories. They explain and describe new information in their own words. They also interpret information from diagrams, charts and graphs.

In second and third grades children improve their word-recognition and word-study skills and develop fluency in their ability to read quickly and accurately. These years also are the time to extend comprehension and vocabulary knowledge and to refine writing and spelling skills.

It is critical that children are up to "reading speed" by the end of third grade. Children who fail to make good progress in reading by the time they enter fourth grade are likely to have trouble in the upper grades and may drop out of school before graduating.

The following are lists of some accomplishments that you can expect of your child by the end of second and third grade. These lists are based on research in the fields of reading, early childhood education and child development. Remember, though, that children don't develop and learn at the same pace and in the same way. Your child may be more advanced or need more help than others in her age group. You are, of course, the best judge of your child's abilities and needs. You should view these accomplishments as guidelines and not as hard-and-fast rules. If you have concerns or questions about your child's reading development, talk to his teacher.

<u>WHAT CHILDREN SHOULD BE ABLE TO DO BY THE END OF SECOND GRADE</u>

Phonics and Word Recognition

By the end of second grade a child:

- Can read a large number of regularly spelled one- and two-syllable words.

- Figures out how to read a large number of words with more than two syllables.

- Uses knowledge of phonics to sound out unfamiliar words.

- Accurately reads many sight words.

Reading

By the end of second grade a child:

- Reads and understands a variety of second grade level fiction and nonfiction books.

- Knows how to read for specific purposes and to seek answers to specific questions.

- Answers "how," "why" and "what-if" questions.

- Interprets information from diagrams, charts and graphs.

- Recalls information, main ideas and details after reading.

- Compares and connects information read in different books and articles.

- Takes part in creative responses to stories, such as dramatizations of stories and oral presentations.

Reading Comprehension Instruction

Quality instruction includes teaching children strategies that they can use to get meaning from the materials they read. These comprehension strategies include being aware of how well they comprehend a selection, using graphic organizers, answering questions, asking questions, recognizing the way stories are organized and summarizing.

To teach comprehension strategies, teachers first demonstrate the strategy, tell why it is important, and how, when and where to use it. Then the children practice the strategy until they are able to use it on their own.

Here are some examples of strategy instruction:

- To help children understand and remember what they read, a teacher presents a diagram called a "story map" that shows the structure, or organization, of simple stories. She and the children talk about the story they have just read – its setting (where it takes place), the characters, the problems the characters face, the different events in the story, the resolutions of the characters' problems, and the theme or moral of the story. As they talk, the teacher fills in the story map. After several lessons with their teacher the children are able to complete story maps on their own.

- To help children better understand and remember what they have read a teacher teaches them how to ask themselves "main idea" questions about what they are reading. The class has just finished reading a selection about redwood trees in an informational book. The teacher gives the children several examples of main idea questions and contrasts them with detail questions. He points out that the main idea questions often start with "why" or "how." Then, under his guidance, the children practice asking main idea questions about several more selections in the book.

- To help children understand, learn from, and remember the information in their social studies textbook, a teacher helps them learn how to write a summary. She demonstrates how to write a summary of one of the sections in the chapter they are reading. She shows them how to make use of the section headings and the topic sentences of each paragraph. She then shows the children how to eliminate details. Under her direction, the children work together to write summaries of several sections of a chapter in their social studies textbook. In subsequent lessons the children write summaries of the chapters in their science book. The teacher provides feedback so that children include the important parts of the chapters in their summaries.

Spelling and Writing

By the end of second grade a child:

- Pays attention to how words are spelled.

- Correctly spells words he has studied.

- Spells a word the way it sounds if she doesn't know how to spell it.

- Writes for many different purposes.

- Writes different types of compositions (for example, stories, reports and letters).

- Makes good judgments about what to include in her writing.

- Takes part in writing conferences and then revises and edits what he has written.

- Pays attention to the mechanics of writing (for example, spelling, capitalization and punctuation) in the final versions of compositions.

Vocabulary and Knowledge of the World

By the end of second grade a child:

- Wants to learn new words and share those words at school and home.

- Uses clues from the context to figure out what words mean.

- Uses knowledge of word parts such as prefixes, suffixes and root words to figure out word meanings.

- Increases vocabulary through the use of synonyms and antonyms.

- Can use different parts of speech correctly, including nouns, verbs, adjectives and adverbs.

- Learns more new words through independent reading.

- Explores and investigates topics of interest on her own.

WHAT CHILDREN SHOULD BE ABLE TO DO BY THE END OF THIRD GRADE

Phonics and Word Recognition

By the end of third grade a child:

- Uses phonics knowledge and word parts (prefixes, roots, suffixes) to figure out how to pronounce words she doesn't recognize.

Reading

By the end of third grade a child:

- Reads with fluency.

- Reads a variety of third grade level texts (for example, story books, informational books, magazine articles and computer screens) with fluency and comprehension.

- Reads longer stories and chapter books independently.

- Summarizes major points from both fiction and nonfiction books.

- Identifies and then discusses specific words or phrases that interfere with comprehension.

- Discusses the themes or messages of stories.

- Asks "how," "why," and "what-if" questions.

- Distinguishes cause from effect, fact from opinion and

main ideas from supporting details.

- Uses information gathered and his own reasoning to evaluate the explanations and opinions he reads about.

- Understands and reads graphics and charts.

- Uses context clues to get meaning from what she reads.

Spelling and Writing

By the end of third grade a child:

- Correctly spells previously studied words.

- Independently reviews her own written work for errors in spelling, capitalization and punctuation.

- Begins to use literary words and sentences in his writing, such as figurative language.

- Combines information in compositions from a variety of sources, including books, articles and computer information.

- With assistance from teachers and classmates, edits and revises her compositions to make them easier to read and understand.

- Discusses her own writing with other children and responds helpfully to the writing of other children.

Vocabulary and Knowledge of the World

By the end of third grade a child:

- Wants to learn and share new words at school and at home.

- Uses clues from context to figure out word meanings.

- Uses her knowledge of word parts such as prefixes, suffixes and root words to figure out word meanings.

- Increases his vocabulary through the use of synonyms and antonyms.

- Is able to use different parts of speech correctly, including nouns, verbs, adjectives and adverbs.

- Develops her vocabulary and knowledge through independent reading.

- Explores and investigates topics of interest on his own.

- Uses a variety of sources to find information, including computers.

The main source for this list of accomplishments is Preventing Reading Difficulties in Young Children. For *more information about this book, see the* Bibliography *in the back of this book.*

Some Helpful Terms to Know (Advanced)

Teachers and day care providers might use these terms when talking to you about how your child is learning to read. Some of them are used in this book.

alphabetic knowledge – Knowing the names and shapes of the letters of the alphabet.

alphabetic principle – The understanding that written letters represent sounds. For example, the word *big* has three sounds and three letters.

big books – Oversized books that allow for the sharing of print and illustrations with a group of children.

blending – Putting together individual sounds to make spoken words.

comprehension – The ability to understand and gain meaning from what has been read.

decodable books – Books that are made up of words that contain only the letter-sound relationships that the children are learning, along with a few words that are taught as sight words.

decode – The ability to recognize and read words by translating the letters into speech sounds to determine the word's pronunciation and meaning.

developmental spelling – The use of letter-sound relationship information to attempt to write words.

emergent literacy – The view that literacy learning begins at birth and is encouraged through participation with adults in meaningful reading and writing activities.

environmental print – Print that is a part of everyday life, such as signs, billboards, labels and business logos.

experimental writing – Efforts by young children to experiment with writing by creating pretend and real letters and by organizing scribbles and marks on paper.

explicit instruction – Direct, structured, systematic teaching of a task.

fluency – The ability to read text accurately and quickly and with expression and comprehension.

graphic organizers – Diagrams that visually represent the organization and relationships of ideas in a text.

invented spelling – See developmental spelling.

irregular words – Frequently used words that don't follow the letter-sound relationship rules that children are learning.

leveled books – Books that have been assigned a particular level (usually a number or letter, such as Level 1 or Level B) intended to indicate how difficult the book is for children to read.

literacy – Includes all the activities involved in speaking, listening, reading, writing and appreciating both spoken and written language.

phonemes – The smallest parts of spoken language that combine to form words. For example, the word *hit* is made up of three phonemes (/**h**/ /**i**/ /**t**/) and differs by one phoneme from the words *pit*, *hip*, and *hot*.

phonemic awareness – The ability to hear and identify the individual sounds in spoken words.

phonics – The relationship between the sounds of spoken words and the individual letters or groups of letters that represent those sounds in written words.

phonological awareness – The understanding that spoken language is made up of individual and separate sounds. Phonological awareness activities include work with rhymes, words, sentences, syllables and phonemes.

predictable books – Books that have repeated words or sentences, rhymes or other patterns.

prefix – A word part such as *re-*, *un-*, or *pre-* that is added to the beginning of a root word to form a new word with a new meaning.

pretend reading – Children's attempts to "read" a book before they have learned to read. Usually children pretend read familiar books that they have practically memorized.

print awareness – Knowing about print and books and how they are used.

root word – A word or word part to which a prefix or suffix is added.

segmentation – Taking spoken words apart sound by sound.

sight words – Words that a reader recognizes without having to sound them out. Some sight words are "irregular," or have letter-sound relationships that are uncommon. Some examples of sight words are *you, are, have* and *said.*

suffix – A word part such as *-ness, -able,* or *–er* that is added to the end of a root word to form a new word with a new meaning.

syllable – A word part that contains a vowel or, in spoken language, a vowel sound (*event, news-pa-per, pret-ty*).

vocabulary – The words we must know in order to communicate effectively. *Oral* vocabulary refers to words that we use in speaking or recognize in listening. *Reading* vocabulary refers to words we recognize or use in print.

word walls – Word-study and vocabulary words that are posted on the classroom wall so all children can easily see them. Usually, word walls are arranged alphabetically, with words starting with a certain letter listed under that letter for easy location.

word recognition – The ability to identify printed words and to translate them into their corresponding sounds quickly and accurately so as to figure out their meanings.

The source of the information in this Chapter is a report published by the U.S. Government, National Institute for Literacy and The Partnership for Reading, A Child Becomes a Reader – Proven Ideas from Research: Kindergarten through Grade 3 (Third Edition, 2006), Jessup, MD.

READ ALOUD
BOOK RECOMMENDATIONS

"You may have tangible wealth untold;
Caskets of jewels and coffers of gold.
Richer than I you can never be –
I had a mother who read to me."

- Strickland Gillilan

The following is a selection of outstanding Read Aloud books for babies through young teens. These are classic stories that you and your child can both enjoy. Use these lists as your starting point. Once you have gone through several of these books you'll be well on your way to Read Aloud success.

Please, make a trip to your bookstore or library and get started right away. Just 10-minutes of Read Aloud each day with your child will make a big difference. Happy reading!

Read Aloud Book Lists

The following lists contain a variety of the very best book choices for Read Aloud. There are literally thousands of books out there to choose from, but let's begin with what I believe to be the best of the best. I've chosen them from my own experience, having read them and used them myself.

Many of these are books that no child should leave childhood without reading. They are the stories that make children want to read, talk about them and then hunger for more. These are the books that we must present to our young listeners before they leave childhood. Otherwise, they'll have missed something really, really BIG!

I can't imagine not reading the Roald Dahl books or Shel Silverstein to my own children. So many lasting memories are made from reading together than from sitting in front of a TV together.

Please look through the following list and find a few to read. The one or two you choose today might have a lasting impact on your child. Your values and your chosen character traits can be solidified by Read Aloud. Let's be choosy parents about what impacts our children's lives.

Please note that each age category includes many different levels of reading material. This is done on purpose. I believe a variety of books helps to keep interest in read aloud. Sometimes I just read a picture book to my class. It offers a complete story, start to finish, with pictures to enjoy. Other times we spend our time involved in a lengthy novel. It all works!

Infants

Experts in child development stress the importance of reading to children from birth to kindergarten. I know from being an educator how significant those birth to kindergarten years are in regard to future school success. Naturally, the perfect age for Read Aloud to begin is babyhood. If you are in this position, with a baby on the way or just arrived, you have this Read Aloud door wide open to you. I urge you to go through it as soon as possible. Some parents even read to their unborn child. Either way, a home where words are also presented daily in the form of Read Aloud is insuring future language and reading development success, not to mention the comfort, bonding and nurturing that also occurs.

Although Read Aloud continues to be important as a child grows, the importance of reading to children from birth to kindergarten is critical. Why? Your child can be immersed in the mastery of the language, including listening, speaking, reading and writing, right from the start of their existence. If you can begin this mastery by providing listening opportunities through Read Aloud you are training those little ears to hear language of the written word, not just the world of everyday chatter!

These children, if exposed to Read Aloud, will be getting speech and listening lessons of exceptionally high quality. They will begin seeing books as positive images involving time spent with you. Books will soon be the visual telling them they are about to have you all to themselves. If you are in this position of being a new parent, you have an opportunity to provide your child with the tools to be comfortable, successful and happy throughout their future school years.

Big Red Barn, Margaret Wise Brown

Are You My Mother? P.D. Eastman

Pat the Bunny, Edith Davies

Goodnight Moon, Margaret Wise Brown

Babies, Gyo Fujikawa

Guess How Much I Love You, Sam McBratney

Richard Scarry's Best Story Book Ever, Richard Scarry

5 Little Monkey's Jumping on the Bed, Eileen Christelow

The Going to Bed Book, Sandra Boynton

The Very Hungry Caterpillar, Eric Carle

Maisy's Morning on the Farm, Lucy Cousins

Brown Bear, Brown Bear, What Do You See? Bill Martin

Where's Spot? Eric Hill

Good Night, Little Bear, Richard Scarry

Some Dogs Do, Jez Alborough

Peek – A Who? Nina Laden

Preschoolers

If a baby has had the experience of Read Aloud, preschoolers can thrive on this next stage of Read Aloud, which ideally will lead to preschool chapter books! Once a child has the ability to interact with you during Read Aloud, moving to simple preschool chapter books is amazing. Remember, Read Aloud is always presented above the child's reading ability, so don't let the words "preschool chapter books" confuse you.

One prime example of a perfect preschool chapter book is *Frog and Toad*. It includes simple stories about two friends that will capture your child's heart as well as your own. *Grandaddy's Place* is divided into short chapters. And, there are many preschoolers who would even be ready to listen to a short novel such as *Charlotte's Web*.

Preschool chapter books have the ability to advance the very young listeners' comprehension abilities. Instead of listening to one story, their brains get introduced to a continuing story.

Unfortunately, there isn't an abundance of high quality preschool chapter books. Therefore, you need to be a bit creative in your approach. Try using a longer picture book and shortening it to form multiple chapters. For example, *The Velveteen Rabbit* could be broken into two readings. Ask your preschooler to tell you what happened in the first "chapter" before you begin the second. Use the pictures as clues as you take a first session "picture walk." Talk about it. This helps your preschooler connect the two parts, which leads to an incredible gift of comprehension.

This age is perhaps the age where it is hard to tell who enjoys Read Aloud more, the toddler or the adult. Preschoolers are so energized and excited about almost everything!

Most preschoolers will love crawling up in your lap to listen to a story, especially if presented with no distractions like the TV. This is a perfect opportunity to spend quality time together, just you and your toddler. If you can create a consistent daily Read Aloud time, you will be nurturing that need for consistency and predictability as well as a huge reinforcement of your love for them as you cuddle and talk. This is a wonderful daily bonding opportunity!

Preschoolers love to look at pictures while being read to, so now is the time to really capture their attention with outstanding pictures and text. Those pictures are giving them their imagination a boost so that later they will be able to use their imagination alone successfully. Get them to point to pictures and talk to them along with the reading text. Make them really a part of the Read Aloud.

Color Kittens, Margaret Wise Brown

Llama, Llama Red Pajama, Anna Dewdney

Curious George, Margaret Rey

Little Bear, Else Holmelund Minarik

Stellalunna, Janell Cannon

Olivia, Ian Falconer

The Owl Who Was Afraid of the Dark, Jill Tomlinson

Corduroy, Don Freeman

Chicka Chicka Boom Boom, Bill Martin, Jr.

Rainbow Fish, Marcus Pfister

The Poky Little Puppy, Janette Sebring Lowrey

We're Going on a Bear Hunt, Michael Rosen

No Matter What, Debi Gliori

Harry the Dirty Dog, Gene Zion

Pinkalicious, Victoria Kann

Kindergarteners

The availability of high-quality kindergarten Read Aloud books is excellent. You are now entering the ages where children can follow a short story, see the humor, and beware... request the same story over and over and over again! You will start seeing the beginnings of particular interests. They are often very sensitive to characters and emotions, so always read the story first because know best your child and his or her emotional hot spots.

Kindergarteners love to predict, so stop at various points and ask what they think will happen next. If they know the story well, they are often willing to read it to you, by telling the story in their words as they turn the pages. This is reading for them, and it needs to be praised... as is.

The best Read Alouds for kindergarten have lots of

action, fantastic pictures and a real plot.

This age child likes to voice opinions. Ask them who their favorite character was and then, why! Ask them if they liked the story, and why. Let them talk about the books. It gives them a sense of book ownership and voice.

Children this age like to pick out books to be read. Perhaps they can have a certain number of books each night ready to be read, in a certain location. Not only will they feel important because they made a decision, they will have been part of bedtime choices that perhaps will ease any apprehension about that time.

Alexander and the Terrible, Horrible, No Good, Very Bad Day, Judith Viorst

If You Give A Mouse a Cookie, Laura Numeroff

Charlie the Caterpillar, Dom Deluise

Katy and the Big Snow, Virginia Lee Burton

Frances, Russell Hoban

One Morning in Maine, Robert McCloskey

The Little Engine That Could, Watty Piper

Voices of the Wild, Jonathan London

Lily's Purple Plastic Purse, Henkes

Mike Mulligan and his Steam Shovel, Virginia Lee Burton

Where the Wild Things Are, Mercer Mayer

Make Way for Ducklings, Robert McCloskey

Cloudy with a Chance of Meatballs, Judi Barrett

The Country Bunny, Du Bose Heyward

Owl Moon, Jane Yolen

Daisy Dawson is on Her Way, Steve Voake

The Storm, Cynthia Rylant

The Lion, the Witch and the Wardrobe (Narnia), C.S. Lewis and Hiawyn Oram with illustrations by Tudoe Humphries

We're Going on a Bear Hunt, Michael Rosen

Fireflies, Julie Brinckloe

<u>*1st Graders*</u>

This age child absolutely needs fantastic first grade Read Alouds! As a beginner reader, he needs to be read to above his reading level! First grade Read Alouds would probably include short chapter books, but can certainly be books with many chapters.

First grade Read Aloud stories must be attention grabbers. This will insure that Read Aloud time is a time that your child looks forward to. This is the age when you can really train your child to be a good listener while also generating love for a great story. But again, be very choosy at this grade level. If it isn't an interesting story or subject matter, don't use it.

Here's one more thing to consider, and it's extremely important. Whenever your child becomes a beginner reader you will need to listen to him or her read to you. This might be a favorite Read Aloud book, a daily school assignment or some special request materials. But, whatever it is, LISTEN WITH AWE! Listen as if you have never heard anything so great! This is a critical time in a child's reading development, and he needs unconditional acceptance.

Yes, this early reading can be difficult to listen to, slow and tedious. Remember, this too shall pass, but we want it to pass on to a stage of wanting to read, not dreading it. Choose to experience this temporary stage of reading as a 'gift' to you, for all too soon this stage will be gone.

It is also very important during this stage that you do NOT merely turn your child loose to read on his own while structured Read Aloud time is reduced or eliminated. The start of independent reading is a Read Aloud milestone, NOT a Read Aloud end-point. Your child REALLY NEEDS YOU to continue reading with him every day!

Charlotte's Web, E.B. White

Winter's Gift, Jane Donovan

Ira Sleeps Over, Bernard Waber

Stopping by Woods on a Snowy Evening, Robert Frost

Everybody Needs a Rock, Bryd Baylor

The Giving Tree, Shel Silverstein

The Polar Express, Chris Van Allsburg

Amelia Bedelia, Peggy Parish

Sarah, Plain and Tall, Patricia MacLachlan

Chrysanthemum, Kevin Henkes

The Important Book, Margaret Wise Brown

The Snowy Day, Erza Jack Keats

The True Story of the Three Little Pigs, Jon Scieszka

Frederick, Leo Lionni

Alexander and the Terrible, Horrible, No Good, Very Bad Day, Judith Viorst

Roxaboxen, Alice McLerran and Barbara Cooney

When I was Young in the Mountains, Cynthia Rylant and Diane Goode

2nd Graders

2nd grade Read Aloud time is wide open for a huge variety of books! This age group just soaks up books of all sorts. Poetry can become enjoyable, both rhyming and free verse. Shel Silverstein's poetry humor is often popular at this age. The rhyme is so important as it gives a sense of rhythm to language. Some longer chapter books can be added and enjoyed at 2nd grade Read Aloud time.

Chapter books are perceived by a child as being for "the big kids," so these are very easy to introduce. However, be very, very careful about what you pick. It must be captivating right from the beginning. It can and should be above your child's reading level. Some families select one novel to read to all of their children at the same time! What a family builder! Each day before the new chapter begins, be sure to review what was read the day before. You'll be giving them a life-long reading strategy that will enhance academics in the future.

This is a great time to let your child bring a large book bag to the library and let him pick out some of the books (along with your choices). It gives him a sense of decision making. This is also a great time to let him start a book shelf of his books. Ownership can tie the knot to liking to read.

High Rise Glorious Skittle Skat Glorious Sky Pie Angel Food Cake, Nancy Willard and Richard Jesse Watson

Little House Series, Laura Ingalls Wilder (A beginner book series is also available.)

James and the Giant Peach, Roald Dahl

Indian in the Cupboard, Lynne Reid Banks

Patrick's Dinosaur, Carol Carrick

Cowardly Clyde, Bill Peet

Fantastic Mr. Fox, Roald Dahl

The Boxcar Children, Gertrude Warner

Charlie and the Chocolate Factory, Roald Dahl

Magic School Bus (series), Joanna Cole

Oh! The Places You Will Go, Dr. Seuss

Stellaluna, Janell Cannon

Mr. Popper's Penguins, Richard Atwater

Turtle Summer, Mary Alice Monroe

A Weekend with Wendell, Kevin Henkes

Caddie Woodlawn, Carol Ryrie Brink

3rd Graders

Chapter books, nonfiction books, poetry and biographies make perfect third grade Read Alouds. Unfortunately, this is the age when many parents actually stop reading to their children. They feel that since their child can read, their job is done. Although these children can read by themselves, it is not a time to stop reading to them! It is an important time to find and read great third grade Read Alouds. They still need to hear professionals read, and that is you! They still need to hear material at higher levels than they read. They definitely still need you to read to them!

Third graders are beginning to get involved in other activities. School work, sports and friends become important, as they should be! Finding time for Read Aloud also needs to be important. Finding a time that does not make the third grader anxious or distracted is crucial. Bedtime is usually a good time. I used to read to my youngest son before school, when the others had already left.

A friend of mine who is also a teacher used to call her third grade grandson every night on the telephone and read a book chapter to him. Recently, she started to use her computer and the Internet and now reads to him with 2-way video as well as audio. She makes sure they each have a copy of the book so he can follow along. She is instilling a love of books while creating a lasting memory.

I have had many parents offer to Read Aloud to my class. Some grades are better for this than others, as far as having parents come in to read. As an educator I see third grade Read Alouds by parents very appropriate! Also, bring in the dads. We need to show boys that dads like to read too. I have had parents come in daily to read ongoing chapters of a novel. Some have taken turns, a different parent each day. That way the class has to summarize to the new reader. Great skill! If you offer this option to your child's teacher be sure you've read the book in its entirety.

Mandy, Julie Andrews Edwards

A Dog Called Kitty, Bill Wallace

Island of the Blue Dolphins, Scott O'Dell

Sadako, Eleanor Coerr

Trouble with Tuck, Theodore Taylor

Where the Red Fern Grows, Wilson Rawls

Call It Courage, Armstrong Sperry

The Velveteen Rabbit, Margery Williams

Dear Mr. Henshaw, Beverly Cleary

North to Freedom, Anne Holm

The Owl in the Shower, Jean Craighead George

BFG, Roald Dahl

The Tale of Despereaux, Kate DiCamillo

My Side of the Mountain, Jean Craighead George

The Lion, the Witch and the Wardrobe, C.S. Lewis

The Thing About Georgie, Lisa Graff

Usborne Books (various nonfiction topics)

4th Graders

The grade I have taught the longest is fourth grade, and I have found that Read Alouds for fourth graders must be action-packed. Fourth graders love chapters that end by keeping you hanging. They moan and groan when the chapter ends and I tell them, "We'll find out more tomorrow." Tomorrow comes and I've got their attention by just picking up the book. *Potawatomi Indian Summer* does that beautifully. Unfortunately, it is out of print now, but most libraries still have it on their shelves.

Read Alouds for fourth grade can often capture the reluctant reader if done carefully. *There's a Boy in the Girls' Bathroom* is a fantastic book with a title that was written to get a fourth grader's attention. It will grab your heart. Along with very short chapters, it includes humor and relevance to fourth graders. And, it will encourage a lot of "book talk."

Audio CD's or tapes can be a great option for Read Alouds for fourth grade. However, be sure to listen to it first. It is great for fourth graders to hear many different Read Aloud voices, but not great to turn them off with a poorly read great book. Kenneth Thomasma has written many Indian stories. His first, *Naya Nuki*, is one he recorded on tape. It is always included in my Read Alouds for fourth grade.

Naya Nuki, Kenneth Thomasma

Riding Freedom, Pam Ryan

There's a Boy in the Girls' Bathroom, Louis Sachar

Number the Stars, Lois Lowry

Stone Fox, John Reynolds

Shiloh, Phyllis Naylor

Sign of the Beaver, Elizabeth George Speare

Because of Winn Dixie, Kate DiCamillo

The Miraculous Journey of Edward Tulane, Kate DiCamillo

Classic Myths to Read Aloud, William Russell

My Teacher is an Alien, Bruce Coville

Runt, Marion Dane Bauer

Snow Treasure, Marie McSwigan

Call It Courage, Armstrong Sperry

Lawn Boy, Gary Paulsen

The Thanksgiving Treasure, Gail Rock

Usborne Books (various nonfiction topics)

5th Graders

Read Alouds for fifth grades are apt to vary greatly from one community to another. Your community may include some very advanced literature. It's best to find out by asking your child's teacher what types of books are being used as Read Alouds. Many Read Alouds for fifth graders include novels that might be considered young teen or even young adult.

Fifth graders still love to be read to. They want to be entertained with a fantastic, but not childish story. Gary Paulson has a lot of great books, full of adventure, for this age group. This seems to be a time where you will see a real difference of opinion between the boys and girls as to what they enjoy. Home is the perfect place to focus on your child's reading preferences.

Loser, Jerry Spinelli

Bud, Not Buddy, Christopher Paul Curtis

Maniac Magee, Jerry Spinelli

The River, Gary Paulson

Bridge to Terabithia, Katherine Paterson

White Fang, Jack London

The Giver, Lois Lowry

From the Mixed Up Files of Mrs. Basil E. Frankweiler, E.L. Konigsburg

The Best Christmas Pageant Ever, Barbara Robinson

The Adventures of Tom Sawyer, Mark Twain

The Pinballs, Betsy Byars

Introducing Shirley Braverman, Hilma Wolitzer

Call It Courage, Armstrong Sperry

The Wish Giver, Bill Bittain

Al Capone Does My Shorts, Choldenko

6th Graders

Sixth grade Read Alouds are a great way to stay in communication with your child! Reading books together that are of high interest to them keeps communication channels open by giving the two of you subjects to discuss,. The teen years are approaching and any common interests now will only help in the coming years.

This age group has many distractions, including TV and computer games, to lure them away from more creative and thought provoking activities. Sports take on added importance at this age, as do other friends. Take it from this experienced parent and teacher, they crave being read to, and those that are read to at home stand out in the classroom. Their fluency and background knowledge is usually advanced. And fortunately, there are many novels that are terrific for this age!

I have no doubt at all that young teens can share Read Aloud and that parent/teen relationships can be strengthened by it. I have seen families continue reading together into teenage years. I have talked to teens who would love to have someone read to them, to take the time to read. I have taught teens who could not have been better listeners as we read novels that kept them thinking, were relevant and had a story that contained real world teen issues. The best stories provoke discussion and opinions.

At the very least, read what your teen is reading! Share thoughts as you go on. I know a lot of families reading *Harry Potter*, each with their own copy, each contributing to the discussions. It creates a common bond.

Ask high school teachers and librarians what the best readers are reading. Then go get a copy of that book and begin reading it yourself. In addition, you should consider reading nonfiction together. Your teen should now have an interest in something that you can find in a book. And, you can even use magazine stories for your Read Aloud time.

Read an autobiography of someone together. *Gifted Hands*, by Dr. Ben Carson, is an amazing story that I discussed earlier in this book. It is the biography of a renowned doctor who came from a life of poverty and illiteracy. He is now one of our top pediatric neurologists in the country. Any young adult or adult would love this! Ben was the lowest student in the 5th grade, ready to give up on education. He is now a brilliant doctor because his mom would not give up.

Touching Spirit Bear, Ben Mikaelsen

Jumping the Nail, Eve Bunting

Blackwater, Eve Bunting

The Pigman, Paul Zindel

Summer of My German Soldier, Bette Greene

The True Confessions of Charlotte Doyle, Avi

Olive's Ocean, Kevin Henkes

Gifted Hands, Ben Carson, M.D.

Redwall, Brian Jacques

Chicken Soup for the Teen's Soul, Mark Victor Hansen and Jack Canfield

Hatchet, Gary Paulson

Tuck Everlasting, Natalie Babbitt

Holes, Louis Sachar

Journey to Topaz, Yoshiko Uchida

Surviving the Applewhites, Stephanie Tolan

Reluctant Readers

Don't we wish there was a magic reading lists for reluctant readers! All we'd have to do is get one of the books from that list, give it to our child, and then BINGO, we'd turn him or her into a reader. Unfortunately, it just doesn't work that way. Therefore, I've included a reading list for reluctant readers that should help those who need it.

Every child needs someone to carefully pick out their Read Aloud books. However, the reluctant reader needs you to add an extra measure of tender loving care whenever you're making book selections for him or her. You must select books that you believe will genuinely excite your child, and as a result, cause him or her to want to read more.

Reluctant readers need that one sparkle book that really grabs them, the book they don't want to put down. If that sparkle did not occur at a young age, it gets more difficult, but not impossible, as the child matures. If their peers do not read, that older child can easily succumb to peer pressure.

I once tried everything I could think of to attract one of my students to reading. However, it was all to no avail until I talked to him in depth and discovered a deep-seated interest in aviation. I immediately put a real live aircraft pilot's training manual in his hands and I couldn't get the book away from him. We need to remember that the older reader has such a wide range of reading materials available. We owe it to them to find the right one. It does not have to be a fiction novel.

Reluctant Readers (1st-2nd Grade)

Ira Sleeps Over, Bernard Waber

Lost in the Storm, Carol Carrick

Accident, Carol Carrick

The Climb, Carol Carrick

In November, Cynthia Rylant

Night in the Country, Cynthia Rylant

Fireflies, Julie Brinckloe

Alexander Who Used to Be Rich Last Sunday, Judith Viorst

Harry the Dirty Dog, Gene Zion

No Jumping on the Bed, Tedd Arnold

Reluctant Readers (3rd-4th Grade)

Witches, Roald Dahl

Harry Potter (series), J.K Rowling

Jumangi, Chris Van Allsburg

Falling Up, Shel Silverstein

The Trouble with Tuck, Theodore Taylor

The War with Grandpa, Robert Smith

The Drinking Gourd, F.N. Monjo

A Dog Called Kitty, Bill Wallace

James and the Giant Peach, Roald Dahl

Books by Matt Christopher (sports stories)

Reluctant Readers (5th Grade and Up)

Touching Spirit Bear, Ben Mikaelsen

Jumping the Nail, Eve Bunting

Blackwater, Eve Bunting

The Pigman, Paul Zindel

Summer of My German Soldier, Bette Greene

The True Confessions of Charlotte Doyle, Avi

Chicken Soup for the Teen's Soul, Mark Victor Hansen and Jack Canfield

Hatchet, Gary Paulson

Tuck Everlasting, Natalie Babbitt

Holes, Louis Sachar

Poetry

Our fourth grade classes have been doing an annual poetry Read Aloud program for a local radio station. We get a great response and the kids love reading their favorite poem to the world! Poetry not only makes for great Read Aloud, it is considered to be one of the best ways to hook some reluctant readers!

Give your reluctant reader a copy of Shel Silverstein's *Where the Sidewalk Ends.* His poetry is funny, illustrated, and easily read and enjoyed. I have given it as a gift to the very young all the way up to my favorite senior citizens. It is ageless!

In addition, put some poetry books around the family room or in a basket in the bathroom. Keep one in the car. They are great for quick Read Alouds. Here are some of my favorite books to use for your poetry Read Aloud time!

Where the Sidewalk Ends, Shel Silverstein

A Light in the Attic, Shel Silverstein

Poetry Speaks to Children, Elise Paschen (A CD is included.)

The Oxford Illustrated Book of American Children's Poems, Donald Hall

A Chill in the Air: Nature Poems for Fall and Winter, John Frank and Mike Reed

A Child's Introduction to Poetry: Listen While You Learn About the Magic Words That Have Moved Mountains, Won Battles, and Made Us Laugh and Cry, Michael Driscoll

Poetry for Young People: Robert Frost, Gary D. Schmidt

If You're Not Here, Please Raise Your Hand: Poems About School, Kalli Dakos & G. Brian Karas

A Child's Garden of Verses, Robert Lewis Stevenson

Heartsongs, Mattie Stepanek

RESOURCES AND BIBLIOGRAPHY

RESOURCES

Portions of this book were taken from the following U.S. Government reports and publications:

Reading Tips for Parents (2003). This report was published by the U.S. Department of Education, Office of Intergovernmental and Interagency Affairs, Educational Partnerships and Family Involvement Unit, Reading Tips for Parents, Washington, DC, 2003. This report is in the public domain with corresponding rights of use. The following U.S. Department of Education Staff were instrumental in developing and producing these materials:

Philip Rosenfelt, Office of General Counsel.

John McGrath, Senior Director, Community Services and Educational Partnerships.

Menahem Herman, Director, Educational Partnerships and Family Involvement Unit.

Jacquelyn Zimmermann, Office of Public Affairs.

Linda Bugg, Linda Cuffey, Carrie Jasper, Elliott Smalley and Amy Short, Staff, Educational Partnerships and Family Involvement.

A Child Becomes a Reader: Proven Ideas from Research for Parents – Birth through Preschool (Third Edition, 2006) and *A Child Becomes a Reader: Proven Ideas from Research for Parents – Kindergarten through Grade 3 (Third Edition, 2006)*. These two reports were produced for The National Institute for Literacy, The Partnership for Reading, Jessup, MD, by RMC Research Corporation, Portsmouth, NH. These reports are in the public domain with corresponding rights of use. The following individuals were instrumental in developing and producing these materials:

Sandra Baxter, Director, National Institute for Literacy.

Lynn Reddy, Deputy Director, National Institute for Literacy.

Bonnie B. Armbruster, Ph.D., University of Illinois at Urbana-Champaign (Author).

Fran Lehr, M.A., Lehr & Associates, Champaign, Illinois (Author).

Jean Osborn, M.Ed., University of Illinois at Urbana-Champaign (Author).

BIBLIOGRAPHY

Anderson, R. C., Hiebert, E. H., Scott, J. A., & Wilkinson, I. A. G. (1985). *Becoming a Nation of Readers: The Report of the Commission on Reading*. Champaign, IL: Center for the Study of Reading; Washington, DC: National Institute of Education.

Dickinson, D. K., & Tabors, P. O. (2001). *Beginning Literacy with Language: Young Children Learning at Home and School*. Baltimore, MD: Paul H. Brookes Publishing.

Gopnik, A., Meltzoff, A. N., & Kuhl, P. K. (2000). *The Scientist in the Crib*. New York: Harper Perennial.

National Reading Panel. (2000). *Teaching Children to Read: An Evidence-Based Assessment of the Scientific Research Literature on Reading and Its Implications for Reading Instruction*. Washington, DC: National Institute of Child Health and Human Development.

Snow, C. E., Burns, M. S., & Griffin, P. (Eds.). (1998). *Preventing Reading Difficulties in Young Children*. Washington, DC: National Academy Press.

Learning to Read and Write: Developmentally Appropriate Practices for Young Children, A joint position statement of the International Reading Association and the National Association for the Education of Young Children (Adopted May 1998). National Association for the Education of Young Children, Washington, DC.

www.ingramcontent.com/pod-product-compliance
Lightning Source LLC
LaVergne TN
LVHW051523080426
835509LV00017B/2176